Crepes, Waffles & Pancakes!

Crepes, Waffles & Pancakes!

Over 100 recipes for hearty meals, light snacks, and delicious desserts

Kathryn Hawkins

Good Books

Intercourse, PA 17534
800/762-7171
www.GoodBks.com

First published in North America by
Good Books
Intercourse, PA 17534
800/762-7171
www.GoodBks.com

CREPES, WAFFLES AND PANCAKES!
Good Books, Intercourse, PA 17534
International Standard Books Number: 978-1-56148-520-8; 1-56148-520-9 (paperback edition)
International Standard Book Number: 978-1-56148-521-5; 1-56148-521-7 (comb-bound edition)

Library of Congress Catalog Card Number: 2005029897

Library of Congress Cataloging-in-Publication Data

Hawkins, Kathryn.
    Crepes, waffles, and pancakes! : over 100 recipes for hearty meals, light snacks, and delicious desserts / Kathryn Hawkins.
    p. cm.
Includes index.
    ISBN 978-1-56148-520-8 (pbk) -- ISBN 978-1-56148-521-5 (comb)
    ISBN 1-56148-520-9 (pbk) -- ISBN 1-56148-521-7 (comb)
1. Pancakes, waffles, etc. I. Title.
    TX770.P34H39 2006
    641.8'15--dc22
                        2005029897

Senior Editor: Clare Hubbard
Editor: Anna Bennett
Design: Paul Wright
Photography: Stuart West
Food styling and home economy: Stella Murphy
Production: Hazel Kirkman
Editorial Direction: Rosemary Wilkinson

Reproduction by Pica Digital PTE Ltd, Singapore
Printed and bound in China by C & C Offset Printing Co., Ltd.

NOTES

All the eggs used in the recipes are medium (size 3) unless otherwise specified.

Use either metric or imperial measures. Do not mix the two.

All Tbsp and tsp measurements are level and have been tested using accurate measuring spoons.

The author and publishers have made every effort to ensure that all instructions given in this book are safe and accurate, but they cannot accept liability for any resulting injury or loss or damage to either property or person, whether direct or consequential and howsoever arising.

6041

Contents

Introduction

In my opinion, some of the best things in life are the simplest, and few things could be as delicious and as straightforward as the humble pancake – a basic combination of eggs, flour and milk, lightly beaten together to form a creamy batter, and then cooked in a thin layer to form a golden flat cake. Nothing fancy and no great culinary skill required. Just plain, simple cooking.

This book covers many different types of batter, and by adding extra ingredients and applying different cooking methods, you can achieve lots of variations from a basic recipe. By adding extra eggs and melted butter, you form the basis of a crepe. These are smaller and thinner than a pancake and have a delicate, melt-in-the-mouth texture. If you add a raising agent to a batter, you have a waffle mixture. Waffles are made in special grids or presses which cook the batter so that it is spongy in the center and crisp on the outside. Waffles are much thicker than a pancake or crepe, and have an attractive honeycomb patterned exterior.

My best pancake memories are of my mother's pancakes, which we always had on Shrove Tuesday (or Pancake Day as we called it). My brother and I watched with baited breath and rumbling tummies as the batter was mixed and then cooked. It was quite a show, because she has the knack – which, sadly, I have not inherited – of being able to toss a pancake over and back into the pan, the other side down, to perfection; she is a truly masterful "flipper"! Once the cooking was over, we would sit down together to our pancake feast, and even today, my favorite way to eat pancakes is the way we enjoyed them then: straight from the pan, warm and hastily folded, with a generous squeeze of fresh lemon juice – the tartness of which made you wince – and a fair sprinkling of crunchy white sugar to counteract the sharpness of the juice.

When I was approached to write this book, my first thoughts on the subject were about the pancakes I have just described. Once I got beyond the basics, however, I realized that the sky was the limit and that pancakes are a truly global food. There are hundreds of variations ranging from the plain and simple to the exotic and indulgent; the thin and the thick; and the smooth and the textured. It seems that just about every country and ethnic group has its own pancake speciality: the French have their thin crepes and galettes; the Dutch enjoy thick, plate-sized pancakes and waffles; in North America and Scandinavia you'll find enriched light-batter cakes and waffles too; Russians add yeast to a buckwheat batter to create small pancakes called *blinis*; in southern India you'll find *dosas*, made from lentil flour and topped with chutneys and relishes; in Ethiopia a flour called *teff* is used to make very large pancakes (or bread) called *injera*; and in Scotland, where I now live, thick, soft and fluffy-textured Scotch pancakes are a favorite on the menu for breakfast and tea, spread with butter and jam.

Pancake batter is extremely versatile. The key ingredients of flour, liquid and eggs can be substituted with other alternatives,

and all sorts of extras can be added to the core batter to alter the thickness, texture and taste. Different types of flour can be used to add variation, and to make gluten-free batters. Grated and finely chopped vegetables, nuts and seeds, and cornmeal all add flavor and texture. Raising agents such as yeast, egg white and baking soda make spongy, plump pancakes and the batter can be dropped on to a hot pan to give different sizes. The liquid can be varied, with fruit juice, coconut milk, buttermilk, soy milk and even beer used to flavor the batter. Cream and melted butter can be added to enrich it. So long as you stick to a basic formula for a batter, the ingredients can be interchanged to produce countless variations.

The name Shrove Tuesday, the day on which pancakes were traditionally eaten, derives from the old word "shrive," which means to confess, and in the Middle Ages this was a day for confessing sins and seeking forgiveness for them before the period of Lent began. Since then, throughout the Christian world, pancakes have retained this association. Batters were made to use up stocks of rich foods such as eggs, milk and butter before the 40 days of Lenten fasting began, during which all fatty foods were to be avoided. In France the day before Lent begins is called *Mardi Gras* (Grease or Fat Tuesday). On February 2, Candlemas Day, European Catholics serve pancakes as a symbol of renewal, family life and hope for the future. The ingredients of the batter can be seen to have a special significance: flour is a staple food, eggs represent creation, and milk symbolizes purity.

In the United States, pancakes have been popular for generations, from the traditional thick cakes of

the North to the thinner crepes made famous in New Orleans. Early settlers found a simple batter easy to cook on an open fire, but skillets and griddles now make the job a lot easier. Waffles were one of Thomas Jefferson's favorite imports from Holland, and on a trip to France he returned home with a waffle iron or *gaufrier*. The Pilgrim fathers spent time in Holland en route to America and took Dutch pancake and waffle batter recipes with them.

Pancakes are also associated with superstitions and customs. It is customary in France to make a wish while turning the pancake, touching the handle of the pancake pan with one hand and,

at the same time, holding a coin in the turning hand. French farmers would give pancakes to their landowners as a symbol of loyalty. One peculiarly English tradition, however, is the pancake race. In villages and towns across the country, competitors line up with a pancake pan (complete with pancake) in hand and run a designated course, having to stop and toss and catch the pancake several times en route.

It appears that waffle history dates back a long time before these events: the ancient Greeks used to cook very flat cakes called *obelios* between two hot plates, and this method of cooking continued throughout the Middle Ages. Like pancakes, they were common peasant food in country regions and were made using simple ingredients. Today, waffles continue to be sold as street food, particularly in northern France and Belgium, although modern non-stick electric plates are used as they are much simpler to operate and clean.

Over the past hundred years or so, the biggest development in the world of pancakes has been the growth in the number of creperies or pancake houses. Originating in the French region of Brittany, these establishments have spread across North America and Europe, and offer a wide variety of pancakes in all shapes and sizes.

This book includes plenty of tips and guidance notes on ingredients, equipment and cooking to help you achieve perfect pancakes, crepes and waffles. Whatever your taste, I'm sure you'll find plenty to choose from, and there's something here to suit every occasion – breakfast or brunch, lunch, supper or snack, sweet and savory, main course or dessert – and I hope you have as much fun and enjoyment as I did cooking them when you re-create the recipes in your own kitchen.

Important ingredients

Before looking at the alternatives and additions you can include in a batter, it helps to understand the chemistry and methodology behind the key ingredients and how they should be used.

The word "batter" derives from the verb "to beat," although, ironically, beating should scarcely be done when making a batter. In bread dough you encourage the development of gluten, the wheat protein, by mixing and kneading the dough to improve its elasticity. This is vital to support the structure of the dough when it is baked and gives bread its familiar texture. In batter making, however, the gluten in the flour plays a much lesser role because you want the end result to have a softer, more tender texture. As soon as you start mixing the ingredients together for a batter, the gluten begins to develop, and if you mix it too much, the resulting cooked batter will be chewy and tough. Just remember: the less you mix a batter the better – perfect pancakes, crepes and waffles should be soft, with a "just set" texture.

The texture can be softened by adding other starchy ingredients which contain little or no gluten, such as cornstarch, buckwheat, rice, oats, potato, etc. The addition of egg in a batter also inhibits the toughening of gluten during cooking. Using thick dairy products in place of other liquid means that you can use less flour to create a thick batter, which will cook to give a spongier, more cake-like result. Adding a raising agent, such as yeast or baking soda, produces the same result.

In batter recipes that do not include the addition of a raising agent, the batter should be left to stand after the initial mixing, before it is cooked. This allows the liquid to soak into slightly developed gluten and the starch to swell and soften, as well as assisting air bubbles to rise to the surface and escape.

The cooking period for most batters is brief so that the gluten and protein in the egg don't overcook and toughen. Yeast-enriched batters are left to stand in a warm place to enable the yeast to develop and create air bubbles – these are then trapped during cooking to give a pancake full of holes, with a spongy texture. Adding baking soda means that as soon as liquid is added, the soda reacts and starts to effervesce, forming air pockets. This type of batter should be mixed very lightly and cooked as soon as possible in order to retain as much of the aeration as possible. When extra egg is added, the batter will be richer and softer in texture, and when baked in a hot oven – see the Sausage and bacon popovers recipe on page 146 – the batter is transformed into a puffed up mass which sets quickly on the outside, cooking to a crisp, while the middle remains soft and more pancake-like.

One of my favorite cooking methods is for crumpets (see the recipe for Tea-time crumpets on page 158), as it illustrates just how delightful and amazing the cooking process can be. You start off with a very plain, thick, yeasty batter, which you cook within metal rings set on a griddle or frying pan base over a low steady heat. As the batter cooks, you will see the mixture slowly rise to the top of each ring and stay there as air bubbles come to the

surface, pop and set. In a few minutes the finished result is a perfectly cooked, freestanding, thick, aerated, spongy batter cake. Marvelous!

Now let's take a closer look at some of the ingredients I have used in the recipes. I have divided them into several sections for an easier reference guide.

FLOURS AND OTHER STARCHES

• Plain flour – suitable for batter making and giving consistency and texture to the batter. White flour contains about 75% or less of the wheat grain. Most of the bran and wheatgerm is removed during the milling process, so it has little nutritional value apart from a high starch content.

• Whole-wheat flour – any 100% flour milled from the whole wheat grain. It has nothing added to it or removed, so is more nutritious. Plain, self-rising and strong whole-wheat flours are available. For batters, choose a plain white or plain whole-wheat flour. The latter can be used wherever white flour is used to give a nuttier, more fibrous result. For a lighter batter, use half whole-grain and half white flour.

• Buckwheat – also known as beechwheat, brank, or Saracen corn, is a plant related to the rhubarb. Its triangular-shaped kernels are gluten-free and a natural source of rutin, which is used as a natural remedy for circulatory problems. Buckwheat can be bought as grains (roasted or unroasted) or as a milled flour. When used in pancakes or galettes, the flour gives a fragrant nuttiness to the mixture.

• Cornstarch – this is made from maize, which is soaked and then ground to separate the germ and the bran, and then the starch is extracted. The starch is collected and dried, and is therefore pure starch, containing no gluten. Cornstarch is a fine white powder and has no taste. It is used to thicken sauces and cuts down on the need for fat as it blends to a smooth cream with liquid, unlike other flours. It gives a soft texture to batters.

• Chickpea flour – also called gram or besan flour, this is made from ground chickpeas. Strictly speaking, besan flour is made from yellow split peas or *chana dhal*, but is often referred to as chickpea flour. It is pale yellow and powdery, with a beany, earthy flavor that is more suited to savory dishes. It contains no gluten and is widely used in Indian cookery for binding together savory breads, dumplings, fritters such as onion *bhajis*, and to thicken sauces. Mixed with water it makes a simple batter. Available in Asian stores and health-food shops.

• Cornmeal – also known as maize meal. It is widely used as a staple in corn-growing parts of the world for both human and animal consumption, and is one of the most widely grown crops in America. Unlike cornstarch, cornmeal is a relatively whole "flour" as it contains most of the grain. In the southern United States the golden meal is used to make breads, cakes and batters. Cornmeal has a slightly gritty texture and contains no gluten. It is widely available.

• Oatmeal – simple oatmeals are made by stone-grinding the oat grain into fine, medium or coarse meal. Fine oatmeal is best used for batter making and gives a thick, wholesome texture. An oatmeal batter requires soaking time to soften the grain, and the batter will thus thicken more on standing, so it may need watering down prior to cooking. The true taste of oatmeal develops after it has been lightly toasted and gives a nuttier flavor. Fresh oatmeal loses its flavor quickly, so should be bought in small quantities and stored well-sealed in a cool, dark place.

• Gluten-free flour (ready-made) – plain varieties are available. A ready-prepared combination of gluten-free flours such as rice, potato, tapioca, maize and buckwheat, is suitable for recipes where gluten is unnecessary, and is ideal for batter making. You may find that the flour absorbs slightly

more liquid if the batter is left to stand, so the resulting mixture will be thicker and may require watering down prior to cooking.

MILKS AND OTHER LIQUIDS

• Dairy milk (plain and flavored) – milk helps to make the batter smooth and turns the pancakes brown on cooking. Cow's, goat's and sheep's milk are all suitable. The fat content of milk has an impact on the finished batter. I have used whole milk in the recipes for substance, but some cooks prefer to use half water and half milk. Using a lighter liquid will make the pancakes lighter in texture, so it's down to personal taste in the end. Some of the recipes use the ready-flavored milks available from the dairy section. I prefer these to the unrefrigerated long-life products which I believe have a different taste. These milks add a subtle flavor to the finished batter, which can be enhanced further by serving the batter with complementary food e.g. fresh banana when using banana-flavored milk, and chocolate sauce with the chocolate variety.

• Soy milk – if you have an intolerance to dairy milk or lactose, soy milk is the most frequently used alternative. Made from hulled soy beans, it looks just like cow's milk and is fortified to make it as nutritious. It is available unsweetened and sweetened – usually with apple juice or fruit sugar (fructose). For cooking, unsweetened is best and it can be used wherever milk is called for; it is excellent in batters, and its slightly earthy taste is undetectable in cooking. Soy milk is available in both chilled and long-life varieties. Once opened it should be kept in the fridge and used within 3–4 days.

• Rice milk – a light and refreshing alternative to dairy milk. It is made from brown rice and is cholesterol- and lactose-free, low in fat and has no added sugar, although it does have a natural sweetness. It works very well in batters, giving a light result when cooked. Rice milk can be used with sweet or savory foods.

• Buttermilk – a left-over product when milk is churned to butter. Most of the fat has been removed and other milk solids are gone. Buttermilk has a sour taste and is often used as an ingredient when a raising agent is being used. The acid in the milk, in conjunction with raising agents, helps to complete the reaction to form carbon dioxide and thus produce a good rise. The commercial product, sold in cartons, is usually found in the dairy section alongside creams, and is made from skim milk with added bacteria which give it a sour taste. Buttermilk can be used instead of milk and gives a thicker batter with a clean, fresh taste.

• Coconut milk – full-fat or light varieties are available in cans, both of which work well in batters. This type of coconut milk is not the liquid found inside the coconut, but an extraction from the coconut flesh. It gives a lovely rich and creamy batter with a mild coconut flavor, and can be used in both sweet and savory dishes.

• Cream – adding a few spoonfuls of cream to a batter, in place of some of the milk or other liquid, will give a richer batter. How rich you want it to be depends on the fat content of the cream. All creams are suitable except the clotted (Devonshire) variety.

• Yogurt – you can successfully make a batter using half milk and half yogurt to obtain a thicker batter with a slightly tangy taste. The fat content of the yogurt used will reflect on the consistency of the batter (see Dairy milk).

• Melted butter and oil – butter is added to give extra richness and a buttery flavor in more decadent recipes. Choose an unsalted variety to add flavor and richness rather than seasoning. Oil can be used instead of butter if preferred – olive, sunflower or vegetable are suitable – while a smaller amount of nut and seed oils such as sesame or walnut can be added for flavor. Keep stirring the batter before cooking each batch to ensure the fats are evenly dispersed throughout the mixture – it will rise to the top of the batter when left to stand. Adding butter or oil will also make the batter less likely to stick to the pan.

• Juice – choose freshly squeezed, unsweetened varieties where possible for maximum flavor and nutrition content. Juice is best used on its own rather than with milk as it will curdle the milk, although it can be used successfully with yogurt. It's perfect for breakfast pancakes and for those on a dairy-free or lower-fat diet. Using fresh juices such as orange, apple or pineapple adds extra freshness and zestiness and makes a light, lower-fat batter.

• Stock – in savory batters, you can replace half the milk with cold vegetable or chicken stock for lightness and flavor. For a fish dish, a plain fish stock works well.

• Coffee – strong, black coffee or espresso work very well in a dessert batter when used to replace some of the milk without adding sweetness. If you want to add sugar as well, then you can use 1–2 Tbsp liquid coffee extract in place of a little milk. A coffee batter works very well with the flavors of orange, almond, chocolate and raspberry.

• Beer – using half beer and half milk makes the batter rise up slightly and gives a mild savory flavor. Use a light beer for a mild flavor, and a dark beer for an earthier, yeasty flavor. Beer is best used with savory accompaniments.

EGGS
The better the quality of the eggs you use, the more flavor you will achieve in the finished batter. Use eggs that are as fresh as possible, and preferably free-range or organic for maximum flavor and a good color. All the recipes in the book call for medium (size 3) eggs, unless otherwise stated.

RAISING AGENTS

• Yeast – available fresh, dried and fast-acting. I have chosen to use the fast-acting variety in my recipes. Also called active dry or instant yeast, this variety is widely available and easy to use. Measure accurately, using kitchen measuring spoons, and stir into the dry ingredients first. NEVER try to activate with liquid as this will not work and render the yeast useless. Once the ingredients are formed into a batter, the yeast will start to work. Cover loosely with plastic wrap or a clean cloth, and set in a warm place for about an hour until doubled in size. The resulting batter will be spongy, light and airy and have a yeasty flavor.

• Baking powder – a mixture of alkaline and acid substances which, when moistened, react to produce carbon dioxide gas, which produces a "rise." Commercial powder combines baking soda (an alkaline) and tartaric acid with a dried starch or flour, which absorbs any moisture during storage. Make your own by combining 1 Tbsp baking soda with 2 Tbsp cream of tartar. Always measure carefully, as too much or too little can upset the balance of the recipe. Use this type of batter quickly to capture the air in the finished batter.

• Baking soda – an alkaline raising agent (used in recipes that contain an acid ingredient such as buttermilk or lemon), which produces carbon dioxide gas when mixed with liquid. It should be added just before cooking; otherwise the gas will be lost.

SWEETENING AGENTS

For dessert batters, you will probably want to add some sweetness. All types of sugar are suitable, although artificial sweeteners usually lose their sweetness during cooking – check the manufacturer's instructions regarding cooking with them. Brown sugars will add color and a caramelized flavor, while maple syrup and honey will add a depth of flavor depending on how flavored they are in themselves, i.e. a heather honey will add a stronger flavor than a mild variety such as acacia. Flavored sugars, such as vanilla, will add sweetness and extra taste in one application.

SEASONINGS AND FLAVORINGS

Once you've got your basic batter, you can add extras to it to change the flavor, texture and appearance. A good pinch of salt is an important addition to any batter, sweet or savory, as it brings out the flavors in the finished dish. Ground spices are useful to add extra seasoning, as are finely chopped fresh herbs. Vanilla and almond extracts give sweetness and depth to a dessert batter, and a spoonful of brandy or liqueur can also be added for an extra kick. Freshly grated lemon, lime and orange rind will add a touch of zestiness to a batter. Chocolate can be melted into milk or added whole in the form of baking chocolate chips; cocoa powder can be incorporated with the flour when preparing the batter for a

stronger chocolate flavor. For savory batters, finely grated fresh Parmesan cheese gives a good cheesy flavor. This is the best cheese to use in batters as the hardness means it doesn't melt like other cheeses, and so does not alter the consistency of the batter during cooking.

For texture, finely chopped or ground nuts such as almonds, hazelnuts, coconut or walnuts will give a thicker batter that requires less flour and has an added depth of flavor. Small seeds, such as sesame and poppy seeds, can be easily incorporated into the mixture to add a delicious nuttiness and texture to the finished batter. Large nut pieces or bigger seeds are less successful in batters as they make crepes difficult to fold, although they can be used in large, thick pancakes. Nuts and seeds are better lightly toasted and sprinkled on the finished dish for extra texture. If you are making a thicker batter, then shredded, finely chopped or puréed vegetables can be added and cooked to give thick, more cake-like pancakes, usually too thick to fold but excellent served stacked with sauce spooned over. Mashed banana can also be added to dessert batters.

Equipment

Before you get started, it's worth considering the type of equipment you're going to need for preparation and cooking. As with any task, using the correct equipment will make the job much easier.

The main tool for achieving the perfect pancake or crepe is the pan in which you cook it. Although it is possible to make a pancake in a standard frying pan, the result will be superior if you use a specialist pan. A suitable pan for the job has a smooth base with gently sloping curved sides, and here lies the main difference: the base and curves of a special pancake pan help with even cooking and easier turning.
The sizes of such pans are usually given as the rim-to-rim diameter of the pan, most commonly 7–8in (18–20cm) for crepes and 10in (25cm) for pancakes. I have found it more beneficial, however, to use the diameter measurement at the base of the pan, so you know how big your cooked crepes and pancakes are actually going to be. This is the measurement I have used in my recipes.

There are several options to choose from with regard to pan material, weight and handle. The general rule is that the heavier the pan, the more evenly and quickly the batter will cook. You only get what you pay for, as the old saying goes, so buy the most expensive pan you can afford. In my experience, cheap kitchen equipment doesn't last long and warps, chips and scratches very easily. A crepe or pancake pan should be kept solely for cooking batters and never used for anything else. That way you'll retain the smooth surface essential for good cooking results, and you won't taint your batter with any other food smells, tastes or colors. Below are some of the different types of specialist pans you might want to consider:

1) The most traditional pans are made from cast iron. In France, buckwheat crepes, known as galettes, are cooked in this type of pan, called a *galettière* or *galetoire*. Cast iron is a good conductor and retainer of heat, although it does take a while to get to the right temperature and is quite

expensive. These pans are heavy and long-lasting. You will need to season a cast iron pan before you use it for the first time, but this is easily done: sprinkle a layer of coarse salt over the bottom of the pan and heat gently. Tip out the salt and carefully rub the pan with a little vegetable oil using paper towel, taking care not to burn yourself. The pan is now ready to use and should require little oiling for cooking the batter. It is better not to wash a cast iron pan: simply wipe it clean, and this will help prevent the pan going rusty by becoming unseasoned. If you prefer to wash the pan, however,

then use hot soapy water and dry the pan quickly and thoroughly. Keep it greased with oil to prevent rusting and repeat the seasoning process before using it again. If the handle is part of the same casting as the rest of the pan, you will need a protective glove or hot pad as it will become very hot.

2) Pans made from heavy steel are also available, but make sure the pan has the sloping sides necessary for batter cooking. These pans look good and last long but are costly and require a lot of care. You will need to season the pan, this time only with vegetable oil, and avoid washing it to retain the seasoning. Just wipe it clean and oil it again before storing to prevent rusting. Make sure the handle is well constructed and firmly attached to the pan so it won't loosen or come off during cooking.

3) For ease and safety, you may prefer to use a non-stick pan. Choose a heavyweight pan with a good quality Teflon® or hard, anodized coating. Providing you respect the non-stick coating it will last a long time. Use wooden and non-stick kitchen implements to prevent scratching the non-stick lining and avoid abrasive

cleaners. Check that the handle is comfortable and has a good grip. Make sure it is securely fixed to the rest of the pan for safety's sake.

Electric pancake makers

You will find small table-top pancake makers in most good kitchen shops. The simplest is a non-stick 2- or 4-round plated machine that looks like a toaster. You simply spoon in the batter, put the top down, and after the specified time the pancakes are cooked. These types of machines usually make small, thick pancakes only. For the real pancake enthusiast, there are electric creperie machines for use at the table, often used in restaurants, with a flat non-stick hot plate. Once the batter is poured onto the surface it is thinly spread all over, using a scraper, and left to cook. Some models are slightly rounded on the outside of the pan base and this is lowered into the batter, upside down, to coat it, and then is released and turned back over to cook. Once cooked, the crepe is loosened with a spatula and flipped over to cook on the other side. Always follow the manufacturer's instructions when using these machines.

Waffle makers

For centuries, waffles have been traditionally made in hinged iron presses and are called *gaufriers* in France. The plates that form the waffles range from honeycomb-patterned to richly adorned designs specially made to order – they would often contain coats of arms or symbols relative to their owner. The iron plates are welded on to long handles for easy turning and should be seasoned well before using, in the same way you would season a pancake pan. They are then placed directly on the heat, be it flame or hot plate, and heated until hot. A good trick to tell when the irons have reached the correct temperature is to place

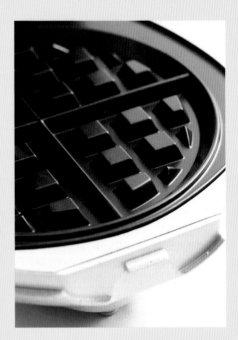

a little water inside before heating; when the steaming stops, the iron is ready to be filled with batter. This method is also a suitable indicator to tell you when the waffles are cooked – when the batter stops steaming, the waffles should be ready.

Nowadays, waffle irons are usually electric (see photo, left). They are fitted with a thermostat and usually a non-stick coating so they don't need greasing. The waffles are therefore easy to remove, although special care should be taken to avoid scratching the non-stick coating. Some models have interchangeable plates so that toasted sandwiches and sometimes pancakes can be made in the machine. If the plates aren't removable, they should be carefully wiped clean once the machine has cooled. Never submerge in water, and always follow the manufacturer's instructions for cooking and cleaning.

OTHER UTENSILS

There are several kitchen tools and utensils that make life easier when you're making and cooking batter. A set of kitchen measuring spoons is vital for getting your quantities right. I have found a small-headed wire whisk a quick and efficient way to incorporate the flour and liquid together without over-beating. The result is smooth and creamy. I think there is a danger of over-mixing if you use an electric food mixer or blender, but it's a matter of personal preference.

When it comes to pouring the batter into the pan, I use a small measuring cup – ⅔ cup (150ml) capacity – with a nicely pointed spout, which is handy and gives greater accuracy. In the past I have used measuring spoons and cups, and a ladle with a spout, but the measuring cup, for me, is the best way to be consistent. If you are using a non-stick pan, then you will need a good-quality non-stick or toughened plastic spatula for turning the pancake, unless you are masterful with your flipping action! For turning a crepe or small pancake, you may find a slim plastic spatula easier. If you're trying something fancy, you may want to contain thick batters within metal rings or cutters (the batter has to be thick; otherwise it will run out underneath the ring). Remember to grease them well so that they can be easily removed. I have also used novelty egg-poaching rings to cook pancakes, such as heart-shaped ones for Valentine's Day.

The perfect batter

There are several hints and tips to take into account when making a batter, but if you follow this step-by-step guide, you should be able to produce faultless pancakes, crepes and waffles galore to the envy of your friends and the delight of your loved ones. It is a universal truth that the first pancake or crepe you make from a batch of batter is usually a failure. I have not managed to figure out exactly why this happens, so I regard this phenomenon as the cook's privilege and a way of ensuring the batter tastes okay!

Basic pancake batter

This will produce the most traditional of all pancakes, plain and simple, but full of flavor and mouth-wateringly soft in texture. The same principles apply, whatever type of flour or liquid you are using.

Makes 8 pancakes

1 cup (125g) **plain flour**
1 **pinch salt**
1 **egg**
1¼ cups (ml) **milk**
Vegetabl

Combine t flo and salt in a bowl; make he the center and break in egg. Add half the milk and gradually work into the flour using a whisk. Beat lightly until well combined and smooth – too much whisking causes the gluten in the flour to develop and will make the finished batter chewy. Add the remaining milk gradually, whisking gently until the batter has the consistency of light cream.

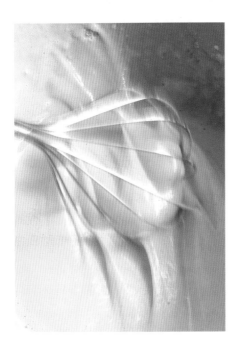

Transfer to a batter bowl, cover loosely and leave in a cool place for 30 minutes. Pancakes made immediately, without standing, will be lighter in texture and have a bubbly surface. On standing, the batter may begin to separate, so stir gently before using. If you leave it for a longer time, the batter may start to thicken and you will need to water it down again to achieve the correct consistency. Never leave the batter longer than 1 hour unless covered and refrigerated; otherwise it will start to ferment.

Lightly brush a medium frying pan – 8in (20cm) diameter base – with vegetable oil and heat until hot.

Pour away any excess oil – the pan should be practically dry. The cooking temperature is important in order to achieve a good finished texture. To gauge the correct temperature for cooking, drop a tiny amount of water onto the surface of the pan. If the drops stay in place, the pan isn't hot enough; if they disappear immediately it is too hot; but when they sizzle and spit across the surface, the pan is ready.

Holding the pan, pour in about 4 Tbsp batter into the middle of the pan, then tilt the pan from side to side so the batter runs into a thin, even layer across the bottom of the pan.

Place the pan over moderate heat and cook for about 1½ minutes, or until the pancake browns around the edges and begins to curl away from the pan. Slide a palette knife under the pancake and flip it over. Brown the underside of the pancake for a further minute.

Turn the pancake out onto a wire rack lined with a clean tea towel and baking parchment. Fold the paper and towel over the pancake to keep it moist. Continue to make a further 7 pancakes, re-oiling the pan as necessary and stacking the cooked pancakes between sheets of parchment until you are ready to serve. Pancakes will keep warm like this while you cook the remaining batter, but if you want to keep them warm for longer, transfer them, still layered up, to a heatproof plate. Cover with foil and place over a pan of gently simmering water or in the oven at a low (keep warm) setting.

TIPS:

- **For gluten-free pancakes** replace the plain flour with gluten-free flour.

- **For whole-wheat pancakes** replace the plain flour with whole-wheat flour or use half plain and half whole-wheat.

- **For a herbed batter** add 4 Tbsp freshly chopped herbs of your choice, such as parsley, chives, dill, marjoram, oregano or sage.

- **To halve the batter quantity** simply halve all of the ingredient quantities. Beat the egg on its own in a bowl and then judge a half quantity.

- **For flavored batters** stir the batter before making a new pancake in order to distribute the added ingredients evenly.

Basic crepe batter

This produces a smaller, more refined pancake, rich and deliciously tender. Add the sugar to the batter if serving with a sweet filling.

Makes 12 crepes

1 cup (125g) **plain flour**
2 Tbsp (30g) **extra-fine sugar (optional)**
1 pinch **salt**
2 **whole eggs**
2 **egg yolks**
1¼ cups (300ml) **milk**
⅓ cup (75g) **unsalted butter,** melted

Combine the flour, sugar, if using, and salt in a bowl. Make a well in the center, break in the eggs, then add the extra yolks. Add half the milk and gradually work into the flour using a whisk. Beat lightly until smooth, but don't over-mix.

Add the remaining milk gradually, whisking gently until it is well combined. Transfer to a batter bowl, cover loosely and leave in a cool place for 30 minutes. Stir ¼ cup (60g) melted butter into the batter before using.

Lightly brush a small frying pan – 6in (15cm) base diameter – with a little of the remaining butter and heat until hot. Holding the pan, pour in about ¼ cup (50ml) batter and tilt the pan from side to side so that the batter runs into a thin, even layer across the bottom of the pan.

Place the pan over moderate heat and cook for about 1 minute, or until the crepe browns around the edges and begins to curl away from the pan. Slide a palette knife under the crepe and flip it over. Brown the underside for a further minute.

Turn out on to a wire rack lined with a clean tea towel and baking parchment. Fold the paper and towel over the crepe to keep it moist. Continue to make a further 11 crepes, brushing the pan with melted butter as necessary, gently stirring the batter each time it is used, and stacking the cooked crepes between sheets of parchment until you are ready to serve.

Basic waffle batter

This batter contains the raising agent baking soda, so use the batter as soon as possible to ensure that the airy, spongy texture is retained. Add the extra-fine sugar if serving with a sweet topping.

Makes 12 waffles

2 cups (250g) **plain flour**
½ tsp **baking soda**
½ tsp **salt**
2 Tbsp (30g) **extra-fine sugar (optional)**
1 **egg**, separated
1¼ cups (100ml) **milk**
¼ stick (30g) **unsalted butter,** melted

Prepare and preheat the waffle irons or waffle machine as directed. Combine the flour with the baking soda, salt and sugar, if using, in a bowl and make a well in the center. Add the egg yolk and milk, and gradually work into the flour using a whisk. Beat gently until smooth. Carefully stir in the melted butter.

In a grease-free bowl, whisk the egg white until stiff and carefully fold into the batter using a large metal spoon.

Pour over enough batter, to ensure that the moulded surface of the lower plates are covered sufficiently (for an electric plate you will need about 3 Tbsp for each plate). Close the irons or lid and cook until the waffles are just brown on the outside, about 3 minutes. When the waffles are ready, remove them with a two-pronged fork or a wooden skewer, taking care not to scratch the non-stick coating. Place on a wire rack lined with a clean tea towel and baking parchment. Fold the paper and towel over the waffle to keep it moist. Continue to make waffles, about 12 in total, stacking the cooked waffles between sheets of parchment, until you are ready to serve.

PRACTICAL TIPS

STORING COOKED PANCAKES, CREPES AND WAFFLES

If you can manage not to eat all the pancakes right away, or if you want to cook them ahead, then stack them as described but allow them to cool completely. Wrap and store in the fridge for up to 3 days. To freeze them after cooling, place the stack in a freezer bag and seal well. Alternatively, wrap well in foil or place in a sealed freezer-proof container. Freeze for up to 3 months. Defrost overnight in the refrigerator. To reheat, divide into two stacks and place on a baking sheet lined with baking parchment. Cover with foil and place in a preheated oven at 375°F/190°C for about 8 minutes, until piping hot.

SERVING SUGGESTIONS

Pancakes and crepes are usually prepared in advance and then filled just before serving. They retain heat well and, if covered correctly, won't dry out, therefore giving you time to fill and fold them to order. There are several ways to present pancakes, depending on what you are serving them with. The easiest way is a simple stack, then everyone can help themselves and eat them as they want – the more you make, the more impressive the pancakes will look. This works very well with the smaller, thicker pancakes.

Larger, thinner pancakes look great tightly rolled into long cigar shapes and piled on top of each other in a pyramid. Simply folding in half then in half again makes pancakes easier to eat and also provides a triangular pocket for a filling. Other ways of filling

include laying the pancake out flat and arranging the filling down the middle, and then neatly rolling up the sides to form a thick sausage shape. For something a bit more substantial, place the filling in the center of a flat pancake, fold two opposite sides up and over the filling, then fold up the other two sides. Turn upside down to make a neat parcel and serve. As soon as your pancakes or crepes are filled or topped, serve them quickly to enjoy their true texture before it softens further.

Waffles are traditionally eaten hot, sprinkled with sugar and accompanied by whipped cream and jam. In France, they are sometimes filled with praline-type mixtures. Nowadays they are frequently served stacked, with all sorts of sweet and savory fillings, and drizzled with flavored syrups. They can be toasted after cooking to give added crispness or, for added flavor and color, pressed onto a hot griddle to char lightly. Always serve as quickly as possible once topped to avoid the waffle becoming soft.

Breakfast & brunch

Breakfast is probably my favorite meal of the day. If it's an early one then I'll just have juice and some fruit, followed by a snack later in the morning. But if it's later or even brunch-time, I usually want something more substantial, and pancakes and waffles are a frequent favorite.

For the health-conscious, you could try zingy Orange juice pancakes filled with a citrus fruit salad, or Cinnamon waffles topped with a mildly spiced dried fruit compôte. If you've got friends or family staying, what could be nicer than to serve them up a pancake or waffle feast for breakfast? You can all dive into Deep-pan bacon and apple pancakes, served with lashings of maple syrup. Or a sky-high pile of Lemon and sultana buttermilk pancakes, accompanied by creamy yogurt and some fresh fruit salad. Impressive to look at, great to eat, and what's more, easy to cook!

For days when you have some extra time on your hands, spoil yourself with a breakfast of Sausage- and egg-filled crepes – perfect for a lazy Sunday.

Breakfast waffle sandwich

Hearty

This breakfast dish uses a classic combination of bacon and eggs. It is filling and will keep you going all morning.

Serves 6

1 quantity **Basic waffle batter (see page 25),** unsweetened
12 strips **lean, unsmoked back bacon,** trimmed
6 **eggs**
Salt and freshly ground black pepper
2 Tbsp **finely chopped chives**

Prepare and cook the waffle batter (see page 25) to make 12 waffles. Keep warm. Preheat the broiler to a medium-to-hot setting. Arrange the bacon on the broiler rack and cook the bacon for about 3 minutes on each side until lightly golden and cooked through. Drain, cover and keep warm.

Meanwhile, poach the eggs. Half-fill a deep medium-sized frying pan with boiling water and bring to a gentle simmer. Carefully break the eggs into the pan, keeping them as separate as possible, and simmer gently for about 5 minutes or until cooked to your liking. Spoon the hot water over the eggs to cook the yolk as it simmers.

To serve, place a waffle on a warm plate and top with two rashers of bacon and a poached egg. Season to taste, sprinkle with chives and top with another waffle.

Breakfast waffle sandwich

Vegetarian waffle stack

Healthy

Mushrooms and tomatoes are popular breakfast foods and are a good foil for these tasty, potato-enriched waffles.

Serves 6

1 quantity **Basic waffle batter (see page 25),** unsweetened
Scant 1 cup (125g) **cooked, cold, finely mashed potato**
6 **flat or field mushrooms,** peeled and thickly sliced
4 **beef tomatoes,** thickly sliced
1 Tbsp **olive oil**
6 **eggs**
Salt and freshly ground black pepper
2 Tbsp **finely chopped parsley**

Prepare the waffle batter (see page 25), folding in the mashed potato as you add the melted butter, then cook as directed and keep warm. Preheat the broiler to a medium-to-hot setting. Arrange the mushrooms and tomatoes on the broiler rack and brush lightly with olive oil. Cook for about 3 minutes on each side, until lightly golden and just tender. Drain, cover and keep warm.

Meanwhile, poach the eggs. Half-fill a deep medium-sized frying pan with boiling water and bring to a gentle simmer. Carefully break the eggs into the pan, keeping them as separate as possible, and simmer gently for about 5 minutes or until cooked to your liking. Spoon the hot water over the eggs to cook the yolk as it simmers.

To serve, arrange a waffle on a warm plate and top with a few slices of mushroom and tomato. Place another waffle on top and place a poached egg on the top waffle. Season to taste and sprinkle with parsley.

Oatmeal pancakes with raspberries

Sweet

If you like oatmeal, you'll love these pancakes. If you have time, make the batter the night before.

Serves 6

1½ cups (180g) **plain flour**
Scant 1 cup (90g) **fine oatmeal**
½ tsp **salt**
1½ cups (350ml) **buttermilk**
¼ stick (30g) **unsalted butter**
1½ cups (350g) **raspberries, defrosted if frozen**
Runny honey to taste
2 Tbsp **toasted rolled oats**

Combine the flour, oatmeal and salt in a bowl. Make a well in the center. Add the buttermilk and work it in using a whisk. Beat until smooth – the mixture will be thick. Add sufficient water, whisking all the time until the mixture becomes looser, but thicker than a traditional pancake batter. Cover and leave in a cool place for at least 1 hour to soften the oatmeal. Stir before using.

Heat a little butter in a large frying pan until bubbling, tilting the pan to coat the sides. Ladle 3 Tbsp batter into the pan to form a pancake about 4in (10cm) in diameter. Cook over low-to-moderate heat for about 2½ minutes until the pancake browns. Slide a palette knife under the pancake and flip. Brown the underside of the pancake for a further 2 minutes. The pancake should be soft in the middle.

Turn the pancake out onto a wire rack lined with a clean tea towel and baking parchment. Fold the paper and towel over the pancake. Repeat to make 12 pancakes, re-buttering the pan as necessary and stacking the cooked pancakes between sheets of parchment.

Arrange two pancakes per person on a plate, then top with raspberries and runny honey to taste. Sprinkle with toasted oats and serve warm.

Lemon and sultana buttermilk pancakes

Lemon and sultana buttermilk pancakes
Zesty

These pancakes are also good served cold with butter.

Serves 4

1 cup (125g) **plain flour**
2 tsp **baking powder**
½ tsp **baking soda**
1 Tbsp **extra-fine sugar**
2 **eggs**, separated
1 cup (250ml) **buttermilk**
Finely grated rind of
  1 **small lemon**
⅓ cup (60g) **sultanas or
  golden raisins**
¼ stick (30g) **unsalted butter**

To serve:
Plain yogurt
Maple syrup

Sift the flour, baking powder, baking soda and sugar into a bowl. Make a well in the center. Add the egg yolks, pour in the buttermilk and gradually whisk into the flour. Beat until thick and smooth but don't over-mix.

In a grease-free bowl, whisk the egg whites until stiff and, using a large metal spoon, carefully fold into the batter together with the lemon rind and sultanas.

Heat a little butter in a large frying pan until bubbling, tilting the pan to coat the sides. Ladle 4 Tbsp batter into the pan to form a thick pancake about 4in (10cm) in diameter. Cook over low-to-moderate heat for about 2½ minutes until bubbles appear on the surface. Slide a palette knife under the pancake and flip. Brown the underside of the pancake for 2½ minutes. The pancake should puff up and thicken.

Turn the pancake out onto a wire rack lined with a clean tea towel and baking parchment. Fold the paper and towel over the pancake. Repeat to make eight pancakes. Re-butter the pan as necessary and stack the cooked pancakes between sheets of parchment. Serve with yogurt and maple syrup.

Deep-pan bacon and apple pancakes
Salty sweet

I first had these pancakes on a visit to Holland. They were
served in a huge stack with a pitcher of dark maple syrup,
and both soon disappeared!

Serves 4

1 quantity **Basic pancake batter (see page 22)**, unsweetened
½ stick (60g) **unsalted butter**
2 **tart eating apples (e.g. Granny Smith)** peeled,
   cored and cut into thin slices
6 strips **smoked bacon**, trimmed and sliced

To serve:
Maple syrup

Prepare the pancake batter (see page 22), and set aside while
you prepare the apples and bacon. Melt the butter in a large
frying pan until bubbling and add the apple slices and bacon.
Cook, stirring, over moderate heat for about 5 minutes until lightly
brown and just softened.

Transfer a quarter of the apple and bacon mixture to a small
crepe pan – 6in (15cm) base diameter – and heat until sizzling.
Pour over a quarter of the batter and continue to cook for about
6 minutes until set. Loosen with a palette knife and slide it
underneath. Flip the pancake over and continue to cook for a
further 2 minutes until golden and cooked through. The outside
should be crisp while the inside stays soft and doughy. Keep
warm while you make a further three pancakes. Serve warm with
maple syrup.

Deep-pan bacon and apple pancakes

Orange juice pancakes

Citrussy

A variation on the basic pancake batter using orange juice in place of milk – excellent if you are on a milk-free diet.

Serves 4

1 quantity **Basic pancake batter (see page 22)**, made using whole-wheat flour and freshly squeezed orange juice in place of milk
1 Tbsp **vegetable oil**
1 **pink grapefruit**
1 **white grapefruit**
4 **medium oranges**
1–2 Tbsp **light brown sugar** (optional)

Prepare and cook the pancake batter (see page 22), using whole-wheat flour instead of plain flour and orange juice instead of milk, and keep warm until you are ready to serve.

Using a sharp knife, slice the tops and bottoms off the grapefruits and oranges. Slice off the peel, taking away as much of the white pith as possible. Holding each fruit over a bowl, cut in between the segments and let the flesh drop into the bowl along with the juices. Sprinkle with sugar, if using, then cover and chill until required.

Serve two pancakes per person, filled with the tangy citrus salad.

Sausage- and egg-filled crepes

Sophisticated

Treat loved ones to a posh breakfast with these buttery delicacies. You can always opt for vegetarian sausages.

Serves 4

1 quantity **Basic crepe batter (see page 24),** unsweetened
6 **good-quality thick pork and herb sausages,** cut in half lengthways
8 **eggs**
4 Tbsp **milk**
2 Tbsp **light cream**
Salt and freshly ground black pepper
1 tsp finely chopped **fresh sage** or ¼ tsp **dried sage**
1 Tbsp (15g) **unsalted butter**

To serve:
Grilled tomatoes

Prepare and cook the crepe batter (see page 24) and keep warm until you are ready to serve.

Preheat the broiler to a medium-to-hot setting and arrange the halved sausages on the broiler rack. Cook for about 5 minutes on each side, depending on thickness, until cooked through. Drain and keep warm.

Beat the eggs, milk and cream together in a mixing bowl until well mixed. Season lightly and add the sage. Melt the butter in a medium saucepan until bubbling and add the beaten egg. Cook over gentle heat, stirring, until the egg begins to thicken and scramble, and until cooked to your liking.

To serve, carefully wrap half a sausage and a spoonful of scrambled egg into each crepe, and serve three per person. Serve with grilled tomatoes.

Cinnamon waffles with fruit compôte

Sweetly spiced

This recipe is ideal for milk-free and gluten-free diets, and it tastes so good that no one will feel they're missing out!

Serves 6

3 cups (500g) **mixed no-soak dried apricots, prunes and figs**
½ cup (90g) **dried apple rings or slices**
2 cups (450ml) **unsweetened apple juice**
1 **cinnamon stick**, broken
1 quantity **Basic waffle batter (see page 25),** sweetened and prepared with gluten-free flour, soy milk and vegan margarine
1 tsp **ground cinnamon**

To serve:
Soy yogurt (optional)

First make the compôte. Put the dried fruit in a saucepan and pour over the apple juice. Add the cinnamon stick, bring to a boil, cover and simmer gently for 30 minutes until the fruit is plump and tender. Set aside until you are ready to serve. Discard the cinnamon stick before serving.

Prepare the waffle batter (see page 25), using gluten-free flour and soy milk, and adding the ground cinnamon to the batter. Replace the butter with vegan margarine and cook as directed. Keep warm until you are ready to serve.

To serve, arrange two waffles on warmed serving plates and spoon over the warm fruit compôte, reheating if necessary. Serve with soy yogurt if liked.

■ *This batter is slightly runnier than the batter prepared with traditional ingredients, so you will notice that the waffles are slightly thinner.*

Cinnamon waffles with fruit compôte

Toasted waffles with poached apricots

Sugar and spice

Giving these sweet waffles a buttery sugar crust prevents them from soaking up too much fruit juice, so you can enjoy both soft fruit and crisp waffles in the same mouthful.

Serves 6

1 quantity **Basic waffle batter (see page 25)**, sweetened
3⅓ cups (550g) **no-soak dried apricots**
2 cups (450ml) **freshly squeezed orange juice**
1 quantity **Sweet spiced butter (see page 163)**, melted
3 Tbsp **demerara or golden granulated sugar**

To serve:
Thick yogurt (optional)

Prepare and cook the waffle batter (see page 25) and keep warm while you poach the apricots.

Put the apricots in a saucepan and pour over the orange juice. Bring to a boil, cover and simmer gently for 30 minutes until plump and tender. Drain and set aside.

Preheat the broiler to a hot setting. Line the broiler rack with foil and arrange the waffles on top. Brush each waffle generously with the melted spiced butter and sprinkle with sugar. Toast for about 1 minute until golden and bubbling. Serve two waffles per person with the poached apricots spooned on top. Accompany with thick yogurt if liked.

Honey and muesli pancakes

Moreish

The muesli requires pre-soaking so you could start this recipe the night before. Try serving with yogurt, honey and banana.

Serves 4–6

1 cup (125g) **plain flour**
2 tsp **baking powder**
½ tsp **baking soda**
1 Tbsp **thick honey, plus extra to serve**
2 **medium eggs,** separated
Scant 1 cup (200ml) **milk**
Generous ½ cup (60g) **sugar-free muesli,** soaked overnight in
    ½ cup (125ml) **unsweetened apple juice**
¼ stick (30g) **unsalted butter**

Sift the flour, baking powder and soda into a bowl and make a well in the center. Add the honey and egg yolks, and pour in the milk. Gradually work into the flour using a whisk and then beat until thick and smooth, but don't over-mix.

Whisk the egg whites until stiff and carefully fold into the batter using a large metal spoon, along with the pre-soaked muesli.

Heat a little butter in a large frying pan until bubbling, tilting the pan to coat the sides. Ladle 4 Tbsp batter to form a thick pancake about 4in (10cm) in diameter. Cook over low-to-moderate heat for about 2½ minutes until bubbles appear on the surface. Turn the pancakes and cook for a further 2½ minutes until golden – the pancakes should puff up and thicken in depth.

Make 12 pancakes in total, re-buttering the pan as necessary, and stacking the cooked pancakes until ready to serve.

Sausage cake and tomato waffles

Savory

Choose cherry or small sweet tomatoes on the vine for this recipe as the natural sugars complement the rich sausagemeat cakes. Remove the stalks before serving if preferred.

Serves 6

1 **quantity Basic waffle batter (see page 25), unsweetened**
1lb (500g) **good-quality sausagemeat**
6 Tbsp **fine cornmeal plus extra for dusting**
1 Tbsp **finely chopped fresh thyme or**
  1 tsp **dried thyme**
Salt and freshly ground black pepper
2 Tbsp **olive oil**
8¾ cups (350g) **cherry tomatoes on the vine**

Prepare and cook the waffle batter (see page 25) and keep warm while you prepare the sausagemeat cakes and tomatoes.

In a bowl, mix the sausage meat with the cornmeal, thyme and seasoning. Divide into 12 and form into small patties about 3in (7cm) in diameter. Dust both sides lightly with extra cornmeal.

Preheat the broiler to a medium-to-hot setting and arrange the sausagemeat cakes on the broiler rack. Brush lightly with olive oil and cook for about 4 minutes on each side until lightly golden and cooked through. Drain and keep warm. Place the tomatoes in the broiler tray and broil for about 4 minutes, until lightly charred and tender. Drain and keep warm.

Brush a large griddle pan with olive oil and heat until very hot. Press the waffles into the pan for about 30 seconds on each side until hot and lightly charred. Drain and serve two waffles per person, topped with two sausagemeat cakes and a few tomatoes.

Sausage cake and tomato waffles

Main meals

Trying to come up with something new and exciting for dinner can be quite a challenge. If it's for a midweek supper, then you don't want to spend ages in the kitchen. And if you're entertaining, you want something that looks good, tastes great and seems impressive, but hasn't caused you too much hassle to achieve. In this chapter I have the answer to a few of your suppertime dilemmas.

I'm sure the family will love the Pancake lasagna – it freezes well so you can make it up in advance and keep it on standby. Waffles are always popular with children, and if you top them with something tasty they can make a well-balanced meal – try the Tex-Mex-style chicken, or Poppy seed waffles topped with ratatouille vegetables.

Pancakes aren't just for serving flat, folded or filled. You can shred them up and serve them as pasta or deep-fry them whole and serve them as a crispy basket filled with salad, perfect for a self-contained starter.

Crepes are an excellent choice for dinner parties and special occasions, and in this chapter you will find recipes that your guests will love.

Chicken and mushroom pancake "pasta"
Alternative

Buckwheat gives a nuttier, earthier flavor to the batter. It is widely available in larger supermarkets, delicatessens and health-food shops. Use white or whole-wheat flour if preferred.

Serves 4

For the pancake "pasta"
1 cup (125g) **buckwheat flour**
1 **pinch salt**
3 **eggs,** lightly beaten
1¼ cups (300ml) **milk**
1 Tbsp **vegetable oil**

½ quantity **Herb and shallot butter (see page 164)**
1½ cups (125g) **small chestnut (or other small) mushrooms,** wiped and sliced
8oz (250g) **lean, cooked, skinless chicken,** cut into strips
1 Tbsp **finely chopped fresh thyme or** 1 tsp **dried thyme, plus extra to garnish**
4 Tbsp **dry white wine**
1 quantity **Basic savory white sauce (see page 162)**
Freshly ground black pepper

For the pancake "pasta" follow the method for making and cooking pancakes (Basic pancake batter, see page 22), but use the ingredients listed left. Keep warm as directed.

For the filling, melt the butter in a saucepan until bubbling and stir-fry the mushrooms for about 5 minutes until tender. Add the strips of chicken along with the thyme and cook for a further minute. Pour in the wine and simmer for 5 minutes.

Gradually mix in the white sauce and stir well until softened. Heat through for about 3 minutes. Slice the pancakes into strips about ½in (1cm) wide and add to the saucepan. Gently toss into the mushroom and chicken mixture and season with black pepper and garnish with fresh thyme.

Chicken and mushroom pancake "pasta"

Deep-pan pancake

Tasty

A cross between a pancake and a pizza. Omit the ham for a vegetarian version. You can incorporate and use up leftover vegetables in this way as well – just chop and add to the pan before you pour in the batter.

Serves 4

1 quantity **Basic pancake batter (see pages 22–24)**, herbed
2 Tbsp **olive oil**
1 **medium leek,** trimmed and sliced
Generous ½ cup (125g) **sugar snap peas,** trimmed and finely sliced
1 **small zucchini,** trimmed and finely diced
4oz (125g) **fine asparagus,** trimmed and cut into short lengths
6oz (180g) **lean diced ham**
Salt and freshly ground black pepper
4oz (125g) **Gruyère or Emmenthal cheese,** grated

To serve:
Crisp green salad

Prepare the herbed batter and set aside.

Heat the oil in a large frying pan – about 9½in (24cm) base diameter – and stir-fry the vegetables for 5 minutes until just tender. Add the ham and seasoning and mix well. Pour in the batter and cook over low heat for about 12 minutes or until set. Keep the heat quite low to prevent the bottom from over-browning.

Carefully loosen the pancake and slide out onto a plate. Flip over, back into the pan, and cook the other side for a further 5 minutes.

Preheat the broiler to a medium-to-hot setting. Turn the pancake back over and sprinkle the top with grated cheese. Cook under the broiler for 3 minutes until melted, golden and bubbling. Serve cut into wedges with a green salad.

Deep-pan pancake

Tex-Mex-style chicken waffles

Tex-Mex-style chicken waffles
Sizzling

I love spicy food and the flavor of onions, so this dish is one of my favorites. Adjust the hot paprika quantity to suit your taste. This is great served with Pineapple and red pepper relish (see page 169).

Serves 6

1 quantity **Basic waffle batter (see page 25)**, unsweetened
2 Tbsp **finely chopped, cooked, dried, crispy onion**
1lb (500g) **lean skinless chicken**, cut into thin strips
½ stick (60g) **unsalted butter**, melted
½–1 tsp **hot smoked paprika**
½ tsp **dried oregano**
1 tsp **extra-fine sugar**
½ tsp **freshly ground black pepper**
½ tsp **salt**
6 Tbsp **sour cream**
6 **pickled jalapeños**, thinly sliced
3 **spring onions**, trimmed and finely chopped

Prepare the waffle batter, folding in the chopped dried onion as you add the melted butter, then cook as directed and keep warm.

In a bowl, mix the chicken with the melted butter, paprika to taste, oregano, sugar, pepper and salt. Heat a large frying pan until very hot and add the chicken mixture. Stir-fry over high heat for about 7 minutes until cooked through and golden.

To serve, pile two waffles on each warmed serving plate and spoon over a little of the sizzling chicken. Top with 1 Tbsp sour cream, sliced jalapeños, chopped spring onion and a sprinkling of paprika.

■ *Use strips of lean beef or pork as an alternative.*

Pancake lasagna

Family favorite

Your family will ask for this dish again and again!

Serves 6

1 Tbsp **olive oil**
1 **large onion,** chopped
1 **clove garlic,** chopped
2 **stalks celery,**
    trimmed and chopped
1lb (500g) **lean ground beef**
1¼ cups (300ml) **beef stock**
1 tsp **dried oregano**
14-oz (400-g) **can chopped**
    plum tomatoes
Salt and black pepper
½ quantity **Basic**
    pancake batter (see
    page 22), unsweetened
2 Tbsp **Pesto sauce**
    (see page 168)
1 quantity **cheese-flavored**
    Basic savory white
    sauce (see page 162)
2 Tbsp **Parmesan cheese,**
    freshly grated

Heat the oil in a saucepan and gently fry the onion, garlic and celery for about 5 minutes until softened but not browned. Add the beef and cook, stirring, for about 5 minutes until browned all over and the juices start to run. Add the stock, oregano, tomatoes and seasoning. Bring to a boil and simmer gently for about 30 minutes until the beef is tender and the sauce is thick. Set aside.

Prepare the pancake batter, adding the pesto sauce to the finished batter. Make four pancakes and set aside.

Preheat the oven to 400°F/200°C. Place half the beef sauce in the bottom of a baking dish, about 12 x 9 x 2in (30 x 20 x 5cm). Arrange two pancakes, overlapping, on top of the meat sauce. Top with the remaining beef sauce and pancakes. Pour over the cheese sauce to cover and sprinkle with the grated Parmesan cheese. Stand the dish on a baking sheet and bake for about 25 minutes until golden and bubbling.

Spicy tomato waffles with pork

Caribbean flavors

The spicy, warm flavors of the Caribbean underscore this dish. It's quite filling so only needs a simple accompaniment – try the Pineapple and red pepper relish on page 169 to carry on the sunny theme.

Serves 6

1 quantity **Basic waffle batter (see page 25)**, unsweetened (using ¾ cup/125g **fine cornmeal and** 1¼ cups/100ml **buttermilk)**
1–2 tsp **hot pepper sauce**
1 Tbsp **tomato paste**
1 Tbsp **vegetable oil**
1 **large onion**, sliced
2 **cloves garlic**, chopped
1-in (2.5-cm) **piece fresh ginger**, peeled and chopped
1lb (500g) **lean pork fillet**, trimmed and sliced
1 Tbsp **finely chopped fresh thyme or** 1 tsp **dried thyme**
½ tsp **ground allspice**
1 Tbsp **dark brown sugar**
14-oz (400-g) **can chopped tomatoes**
14-oz (400g) **can black-eyed beans**, drained
Thyme, to garnish

Prepare the waffle batter (see page 25) using half cornmeal to flour, and replacing the milk with buttermilk. Stir hot pepper sauce to taste and tomato paste into the batter, and cook as directed. Keep the waffles warm.

Heat the oil in a saucepan and gently fry the onion, garlic and ginger for about 5 minutes until softened but not browned. Add the pork and cook, stirring, for a further 5 minutes until browned all over. Add the remaining ingredients and bring to a boil, then simmer gently for about 20 minutes until tender.

To serve, pile two waffles onto warmed serving plates and spoon over the pork and beans. Garnish with thyme.

Prawn and mango pancake baskets
Innovative

Pancakes make perfect food "containers."

Serves 4

½ quantity **Basic pancake batter (see page 22),** unsweetened and made with whole-wheat flour
3 Tbsp **reduced-fat mayonnaise**
1 Tbsp **mango chutney**
½ tsp **mild curry powder**
1 **large ripe mango**
¼ **crisp lettuce e.g. romaine**
¼ **cucumber,** cut into small chunks
12oz (350g) **large peeled prawns,** defrosted if frozen
Oil for deep-frying
Few **sprigs cilantro**

Prepare the pancake batter (see page 22). Cook as described to make four pancakes and set aside.

Mix the mayonnaise, chutney and curry powder together. Cover and chill until required.

Peel the mango and slice down either side of the smooth, flat central stone. Discard the stone and chop the flesh. Place in a bowl. Break up the lettuce and add to the bowl along with the cucumber and prawns. Mix together gently, cover and chill until required.

Heat the oil for deep-frying to a temperature of 400°F/200°C. Line a large metal sieve or frying basket – about 6in (15cm) base diameter – with a pancake so that it moulds to its shape, and carefully lower into the oil. Hold it in place with another sieve or large metal ladle, submerging it in the oil for about 1½ minutes until golden and crisp. Drain and keep warm while you prepare the other three pancakes.

Pile some prawn and mango salad into each basket and serve immediately, topped with the mango mayonnaise and fresh cilantro.

Prawn and mango pancake baskets

Thanksgiving pancakes
Sweet and sour

These pancakes will be thicker because of the added potato in the batter. Replace sweet potato with white potato, if preferred.

Serves 4

1 quantity **Basic pancake batter (see page 22), unsweetened**
Scant 1 cup (125g) **cooked, cold, mashed sweet potato**
1 quantity **Basic savory white sauce (see page 162)**
2 Tbsp **dry white wine or chicken stock**
2 Tbsp **heavy cream**
2 Tbsp **cranberry sauce, plus extra to serve**
12oz (350g) **lean cooked turkey, cut into strips**
2 Tbsp **finely chopped chives, plus extra to garnish**
Salt and freshly ground black pepper

Prepare the pancake batter (see page 22), folding in the mashed sweet potato. Cook as directed but add an extra minute to the cooking time on each side to make eight thick pancakes, and keep warm.

Prepare the savory white sauce as directed, using 1 cup (60g) flour and ½ stick (60g) butter, and stir in the wine or stock, cream and cranberry sauce. Carefully stir in the cooked turkey and heat through, stirring, for about 5 minutes until piping hot.

Just before serving, stir the chives into the sauce and season as necessary. Pile one-eighth of the sauce into the center of each pancake and carefully fold over. Serve two pancakes per person, with extra cranberry sauce and a garnish of chives.

■ *Cooked chicken, ham or prawns would also make good fillings.*

Thanksgiving pancakes

Potato-style pancakes

Comforting

This recipe is based on a traditional potato dish from Ireland, which is made in a large flat cake and cooked on a griddle.

Serves 4

8oz (250g) **potatoes, peeled and grated**
Scant 2 cups (250g) **cooked, cold, mashed potato**
2 cups (250g) **plain flour**
1 tsp **baking powder**
1 tsp **salt**
¼ stick (30g) **unsalted butter,** melted
1 **egg,** beaten
Scant 1 cup (200ml) **milk**
4 tsp **vegetable oil**
8 strips **unsmoked bacon,** chopped
½ **green cabbage e.g. Savoy,** shredded
Freshly ground black pepper and nutmeg

Put the grated potato in a clean tea towel and wring to remove as much liquid as possible. Mix the grated and mashed potato together.

Sift the flour, baking powder and salt into a bowl and make a well in the center. Add the melted butter, egg, ⅔ cup (150ml) milk and the potato mixture. Gradually work the dry ingredients into the wet ingredients, taking care not to over-mix, adding more milk if necessary to form a dropping consistency.

Brush a large frying pan with a little of the oil and heat until hot. Form the potato mixture into eight cakes about 3in (7cm) in diameter. Fry them in the pan over low-to-moderate heat for about 5 minutes on each side, until golden and cooked through. Drain and keep warm.

Heat the remaining oil until hot and stir-fry the bacon and cabbage for about 7 minutes until cooked through. Pile onto the pancakes and serve seasoned with freshly ground black pepper and nutmeg.

Potato-style pancakes

Jambalaya pancakes

Jambalaya pancakes
Creole

I love the flavors of Jambalaya, a hearty meat, seafood and rice dish from New Orleans. The mixture lends itself perfectly to a pancake filling, although I have omitted the rice.

Serves 4

1 quantity **Basic pancake batter (see page 22),** unsweetened, made with 1¼ cups (300ml) **buttermilk**
2 Tbsp **sun-dried tomato paste**
¼ tsp **garlic powder**
1 Tbsp **vegetable oil**
1 **medium onion,** chopped
2 **stalks celery,** trimmed and chopped, and leaves reserved for garnish
1 **small red pepper,** deseeded and chopped
1 **small green pepper,** deseeded and chopped
1 tsp **Cajun spice seasoning**
14-oz (400-g) **can chopped tomatoes**
8oz (250g) **cooked, lean chicken,** chopped
4oz (125g) **large, peeled prawns,** defrosted if frozen
Salt and freshly ground black pepper

Prepare the pancake batter (see page 22), replacing the milk with buttermilk. Stir the tomato paste and garlic powder into the batter, and cook as directed. Keep warm.

Heat the oil in a large frying pan and gently fry the onion, celery and peppers for about 5 minutes until softened but not browned. Add the Cajun seasoning and tomatoes, bring to a boil and simmer for 20 minutes until tender.

Stir the cooked chicken and prawns into the mixture and heat through for about 5 minutes until piping hot. Season to taste. Pile the jambalaya filling onto each pancake and fold over. Serve two per person, sprinkled with reserved celery leaves.

Red beet crepes with smoked fish

Smoky

Cooked red beet gives these crepes a fantastic pink color that's guaranteed to be a talking point. Choose cooked red beet in natural juice, not vinegar, for this recipe. Serve with lemon wedges to squeeze over.

Serves 4 as a main course, 6 as a starter

1 quantity **Basic crepe batter (see page 24)**, unsweetened
4oz (125g) **cooked red beet in natural juice,** drained and grated
12oz (350g) **smoked mackerel fillets**, skinned and flaked
1 Tbsp **lemon juice**
4 Tbsp **sour cream**
2 Tbsp **reduced-fat mayonnaise**
1 Tbsp **mild horseradish sauce**
1 bunch **watercress**, ripped slightly

To serve:
Salad leaves
Lemon wedges

Prepare the crepe batter (see page 24), folding in the grated red beet together with the melted butter. Cook and keep warm as directed.

Gently mix the smoked mackerel with the lemon juice, sour cream, mayonnaise and horseradish sauce. Cover and chill until required.

Serve the crepes while warm, filled with watercress and the smoked mackerel filling. Accompany with a few salad leaves and lemon wedges.

Red beet crepes with smoked fish

Walnut crepes with waldorf-style chicken

Nutty

I like to serve these crepes with a bitter leaf and green apple salad, dressed with honey and wholegrain mustard. The sweet-sour combination works well with this dish.

Serves 4

1 quantity **Basic crepe batter (see page 24),** unsweetened
4 Tbsp **walnut-flavored Pesto sauce (see page 168)**
1 Tbsp **olive oil**
1 **small onion,** finely chopped
2 **stalks celery,** trimmed and chopped,
   leaves reserved for garnish
12oz (350g) **lean, cooked, skinless chicken,** cut into thin strips
4oz (125g) **blue cheese e.g. Stilton or Roquefort,** crumbled
⅔ cup (150ml) **light cream**
Salt and freshly ground black pepper
¼ cup (30g) **toasted walnut pieces**

Prepare the crepe batter (see page 24), adding the walnut-flavored Pesto sauce to the finished batter. Cook as described and keep warm until you are ready to serve.

Heat the oil in a frying pan and gently cook the onion and celery for about 5 minutes until tender but not browned. Stir in the chicken, cheese and cream. Heat through over gentle heat, stirring, for about 5 minutes until the cheese has melted and the sauce is piping hot. Take care not to boil the sauce as it may separate. Season to taste.

To serve, fold the crepes in half and then in half again. Fill each with the chicken mixture and serve sprinkled with toasted walnuts and garnished with celery leaves.

Seafood buckwheat crepe bake

Sophisticated

A luxurious take on fish pie, try serving this dish topped with Pickled cucumber and caper relish (see page 173).

Serves 6

1 quantity **Basic crepe batter (see page 24),** unsweetened and made with half buckwheat and half white flour

4oz (125g) **Gruyère cheese,** grated

1 quantity **Basic savory white sauce (see page 162)**

1½lb (750g) **assorted cooked seafood e.g. peeled prawns, shelled mussels, queen scallops, crabmeat, squid rings,** defrosted if frozen

2 Tbsp **finely chopped fresh dill, plus extra to garnish**

Salt and freshly ground black pepper

1 **egg yolk**

To serve:
Lemon wedges
Salad

Prepare the crepe batter and cook the crepes. Set aside.

Preheat the oven to 375°F/190°C. Mix half the cheese into the white sauce and combine a quarter of the sauce with the seafood. Add the dill and some seasoning.

Fold each crepe in half and then in half again, to form a triangular pocket. Fill each with the seafood mixture and arrange the crepes, over-lapping, in a lightly greased ovenproof gratin dish.

Mix the egg yolk into the remaining white sauce and spoon over the top of the crepes. Sprinkle with the remaining cheese and stand the dish on a baking sheet. Bake for about 25 minutes until bubbling and lightly golden. Garnish with dill and serve with lemon wedges and a salad.

Spicy crab salad crepes

Light and airy

The egg-white batter used in this recipe works very well with sweet and savory fillings. Cook gently so that you maintain as much of the batter's "whiteness" as possible.

Serves 4

4 **spring onions,** chopped
12oz (350g) **crabmeat**
1 dash **tabasco sauce**
4 Tbsp **low-fat plain yogurt**
2 tsp **light soy sauce**
3 **large egg whites,** lightly beaten
4 Tbsp **cornstarch**
8 tsp **vegetable stock or water**
1 pinch **salt**
1 tsp **vegetable oil**
Few **bok choy leaves,** shredded
1 **large red pepper,** deseeded and cut into thin strips
Smoked paprika to dust (optional)

In a bowl, gently mix together the chopped spring onions, crabmeat, tabasco sauce, yogurt and soy sauce. Cover and chill until required.

Put the egg whites and cornstarch in a batter bowl and stir in the stock or water, mixing well to form a smooth paste. Season lightly. Brush a non-stick crepe pan – 6in (15cm) base diameter – with a little oil and heat until hot. Pour in a quarter of the batter, tilting the pan to cover the base. Cook over low-to-moderate heat for a few seconds until just set. Flip the crepe over and cook for a few more seconds, taking care not to brown the crepe. Drain on paper towel, layer with baking parchment and keep warm while you make the remaining three crepes. Stir the batter each time it is used.

Lay the crepes on warm plates and fill with the bok choy, pepper and crab salad. Fold the crepes over the filling and serve dusted with paprika if using.

Spicy crab salad crepes

Salmon and herb waffles

Fresh

A perfect dish for a light spring or summer lunch.

Serves 6

1lb (500g) **salmon fillets**
2 **bay leaves**
Scant 1 cup (210ml) **dry white wine**
1 quantity **Basic waffle batter (see page 25), unsweetened**
3 Tbsp **chopped dill**
3 Tbsp **chopped tarragon**
2½ Tbsp + 1 tsp **cornstarch**
Salt and freshly ground black pepper
6oz (180g) **smoked salmon pieces**
6 Tbsp **light cream**
3 Tbsp **finely chopped chives**
Fresh dill, to garnish

Wash and pat dry the salmon fillets and place in a large shallow pan with a lid. Add the bay leaves and wine, and about 2 cups (450ml) water to just cover the fish. Bring to a boil, cover and simmer gently for about 8 minutes until just cooked through. Set aside to cool. Prepare the waffle batter (see page 25), adding the dill and tarragon. Cook and keep warm.

Drain the salmon, reserving the stock, and discard the skin and bay leaves. Flake the salmon and set aside. Strain the stock through a sieve into a jug, and reserve 2½ cups (600ml).

Place the cornstarch in a saucepan and add a little of the reserved stock. Mix to form a paste, then pour in the remaining stock. Bring to a boil, stirring, and cook for 1 minute. Remove from the heat and stir in the seasoning, smoked salmon, cream and chives, then carefully mix in the cooked, flaked salmon. Return to a gentle heat for about 5 minutes until piping hot, taking care not to boil. Pile the salmon mixture on the waffles and serve with dill.

Salmon and herb waffles

Spinach pancakes with haddock

Spinach pancakes with haddock

Smoky

I was thinking of fish Florentine when I came up with this recipe.

Serves 4

5 cups (250g) **spinach,**
  trimmed
1 quantity **Basic pancake
  batter (see page 22),**
  unsweetened
12oz (350g) **smoked
  haddock fillet**
2½ cups (600ml) **milk**
1 **bay leaf**
1 quantity **Basic savory
  white sauce (see page
  162)**
4oz (125g) **Gruyère cheese,**
  grated
2 Tbsp **finely chopped
  fresh chives**
Salt and ground black pepper
2 **large eggs,** hard-boiled
  and chopped
**Tomato, black olive,
  garlic and basil salsa
  (page 172),** to serve

Wash the spinach leaves
and pack into a saucepan
while still wet. Cover the pan
with a lid and cook the
spinach over gentle heat for
about 5 minutes, until wilted.

Drain well, pressing against
the sides of a colander to
extract as much water as
possible. Allow the spinach
to cool and then chop finely.

Prepare the batter and stir in
the spinach. Make the
pancakes and keep warm.
Wash and pat dry the
haddock and place in a
shallow pan with a lid. Pour
over the milk and add the
bay leaf. Bring to a boil,
cover and simmer gently for
about 5 minutes until cooked
through. Drain, reserving the
milk to make the white
sauce. Discard the bay leaf.

Remove the skin from the
haddock and flake the flesh.
Cover and keep warm.
Make the white sauce and
stir in the grated cheese and
chives. Season and stir in the
haddock and egg. Heat
through gently for about
3 minutes until piping hot
then fill the pancakes with
the mixture. Serve with
the salsa.

Spicy lamb and chickpea waffles

Spicy lamb and chickpea waffles

Warm and spicy

Some of my favorite spices are included in this recipe. The flavors remind me of trips to Morocco and enjoying delicious, slow-cooked tagines seasoned with warming herbs and sweet spices. This is real comfort food for me.

Serves 6

1 quantity **Basic waffle batter (page 25),** unsweetened
1 tsp **mild curry powder**
1 Tbsp **vegetable oil**
1 **red onion,** finely sliced
1lb (500g) **lean lamb fillet,** trimmed and sliced
1 tsp **ground cumin**
1 tsp **ground coriander**
14-oz (400-g) **can chopped tomatoes**
½ cup (125g) **okra,** trimmed and halved
14-oz (400-g) **can chickpeas,** drained
Salt and freshly ground black pepper
Few **sprigs cilantro**
Roasted spiced vegetable chutney (see page 172), to serve

Prepare the waffle batter. Stir in the curry powder and cook the waffles as directed. Keep warm until you are ready to serve.

Meanwhile, heat the oil in a saucepan and gently fry the onion, lamb and ground spices for about 5 minutes, stirring, until the lamb is browned all over. Stir in the chopped tomatoes and bring to a boil. Add the okra and chickpeas, cover and simmer gently for about 20 minutes until tender, adding a little water if the mixture becomes too dry. Season to taste.

To serve, pile the lamb mixture on top of the waffles and serve with some fresh cilantro sprigs on top. Serve with the chutney.

Spinach crepes with mixed mushrooms
Rich

These elegant crepes would make a delicious starter for a vegetarian supper. Serve with a green salad as a main course.

Serves 4 as a main course, 6 as a starter

5 cups (250g) **spinach**, trimmed
1 quantity **Basic crepe batter (see page 24)**, unsweetened
2 tsp **olive oil**
2 **shallots**, finely chopped
2 **cloves garlic**, finely chopped
¼ stick (60g) **unsalted butter**
1 Tbsp **finely chopped fresh thyme**
4½ cups (350g) **assorted mushrooms e.g. button, oyster, chestnut, shiitake**, wiped and sliced
4 Tbsp **dry white wine**
1¼ cups (300ml) **heavy cream**
Salt and black pepper
Fresh thyme, to garnish

Wash the spinach and pack into a saucepan while still wet. Cover and cook over gentle heat for about 5 minutes until the leaves are wilted. Drain well, pressing against the sides of a colander to extract as much water as possible. Allow to cool and then chop finely.

Prepare the batter and stir in the chopped spinach. Make the crepes and keep warm. Take care not to over-cook them as they will be thicker and more difficult to fold.

Heat the oil in a large frying pan and gently fry the shallots and garlic for 3 minutes until just softened. Add the butter and melt until bubbling, then stir in the thyme and mushrooms and cook, stirring, for about 5 minutes until browned and tender.

Stir in the wine and cream and bring to a simmer, heat through for about 3 minutes until piping hot. Season, then fill the crepes with the mixture. Garnish with thyme.

Spinach crepes with mixed mushrooms

Shredded vegetable pancakes

Gluten-free

Experiment with different vegetable combinations. Serve as a starter with Sweet carrot and ginger chutney (see page 171).

Makes 6

1 cup (125g) **gluten-free flour**
2 tsp **gluten-free baking powder**
½ tsp **baking soda**
½ tsp **salt**
2 **eggs,** separated
1 cup (250ml) **unsweetened soy milk**
1 **carrot,** finely grated
1 **zucchini,** trimmed and grated
1 **leek,** trimmed and finely shredded
1 tsp **dried mixed herbs**
Freshly ground black pepper
1 Tbsp **vegetable oil**

Sift the flour, baking powder, baking soda and salt into a bowl and make a well in the center. Add the egg yolks and the soy milk and gradually whisk into the flour. Beat until thick and smooth, but don't over-mix.

Whisk the egg whites until stiff then, using a large metal spoon, carefully fold them into the batter together with the vegetables, herbs and black pepper.

Heat a little oil in a crepe pan – 6in (15cm) base diameter – until hot. Pour in about 5fl oz (150ml) of batter to form a thick pancake. Cook over low-to-moderate heat for 2 minutes until bubbles appear on the surface and the top sets. Turn the pancakes and cook for a further 2 minutes until golden and thick.

Turn the pancakes out onto a wire rack lined with a clean tea towel and baking parchment. Cover the pancakes to keep moist. Repeat to make six pancakes, re-oiling the pan as necessary and stacking the cooked pancakes until you are ready to serve.

Shredded vegetable pancakes

Poppy seed waffles with ratatouille

Poppy seed waffles with ratatouille
Healthy

It is worth salting the eggplant for the ratatouille sauce – it will be more tender and absorb the flavors from the sauce.

Serves 4

1 **eggplant**
Salt
1 quantity **Basic waffle batter (see page 25)**, unsweetened and made with gluten-free flour, gluten-free baking powder, soy milk and vegan margarine
2 Tbsp **poppy seeds**
2 Tbsp **olive oil**
1 tsp **coriander seeds, crushed**
1 **large onion, chopped**
1 **clove garlic, crushed**
1 **large red pepper, deseeded and chopped**
1 **large zucchini, trimmed and chopped**
2 **bay leaves**
14-oz (400-g) **can chopped tomatoes**
4 Tbsp **dry red wine**
2 Tbsp **tomato paste**
1 tsp **extra-fine sugar**
Freshly ground black pepper
2 Tbsp **finely chopped fresh parsley**

Trim the eggplant and cut into small pieces. Layer up in a colander or strainer, sprinkling with salt as you go, and allow to stand for 30 minutes. Rinse well and pat dry with paper towel.

Meanwhile, make up the waffle batter. Stir in the poppy seeds and cook as directed to make about 10 waffles. Keep warm.

Heat the oil in a large saucepan and gently fry the coriander seeds, onion, garlic and pepper for 5 minutes. Stir in the eggplant and cook for a further 3 minutes. Add the remaining ingredients, except the parsley, mix well and bring to a boil. Cover and simmer for about 20 minutes until just tender. Serve the sauce piled on top of the waffles and sprinkle with parsley.

Whole-wheat spinach pancake stack

Wholesome

Gently press the layers together as you construct the stack so that it cooks evenly in the oven and cuts more easily.

Serves 6

1 quantity **Basic pancake batter (see page 22),** unsweetened and made with whole-wheat flour
20 cups (1kg) **spinach,** trimmed
1 Tbsp **olive oil**
1 **bunch spring onions,** trimmed and chopped
1 **egg**
1 **egg yolk**
1 cup (250g) **cottage cheese**
½ tsp **grated nutmeg**
Salt and freshly ground black pepper
¼ cup (30g) **grated mature Cheddar cheese**
¼ cup (30g) **walnut pieces**

Prepare the pancake batter and cook as directed. Set aside until required.

Wash the spinach leaves and pack into a large saucepan while still wet. Cover the pan with a lid and cook the spinach over gentle heat for about 7 minutes, turning the leaves over halfway through, until the leaves are wilted. Drain well, pressing against the sides of a colander to extract as much water as possible. Allow to cool, then chop finely.

Preheat the oven to 375°F/190°C. Heat the oil in a frying pan and fry the spring onions for about 3 minutes until softened but not browned. Mix with the spinach and remaining ingredients except the Cheddar cheese and walnuts.

Layer the pancakes and spinach on a baking sheet lined with baking parchment, with a pancake on the top. Sprinkle with the Cheddar cheese and walnuts and bake in the oven for 20–25 minutes until firm and golden. Allow to stand for 10 minutes, then slice.

Wild rice pancakes with chicken

Indulgent

Wild rice has a good texture and a mildly nutty flavor.

Serves 4

1 cup (125g) **rice flour**
2 tsp **gluten-free baking powder**
½ tsp **baking soda**
2 Tbsp **finely chopped fresh parsley plus extra for garnish**
¾ cup (125g) **cooked, cold wild rice**
2 **medium eggs,** separated
1 cup (250ml) **milk**
¼ stick (30g) **unsalted butter**
1 **large, ripe avocado**
1 Tbsp **lemon juice**
12oz (350g) **smoked chicken,** cut into strips
4 Tbsp **mayonnaise**
4 strips **cooked, crispy bacon,** chopped
Freshly ground black pepper

Sift the flour, baking powder and soda into a bowl and make a well in the center. Add parsley, wild rice and egg yolks, and pour in the milk. Gradually work into the flour using a whisk and then beat until thick and smooth, but don't over-mix.

Whisk the egg whites until stiff and carefully fold into the batter using a metal spoon.

Heat a little butter in a large frying pan until bubbling, tilting the pan to coat the sides. Ladle 4 Tbsp batter to form a thick pancake about 4in (10cm) in diameter. Cook over a low-to-moderate heat for about 2½ minutes. Turn over and cook for a further 2½ minutes until golden. Make seven further pancakes and cover to keep moist until ready to serve.

Halve the avocado and remove the pit. Remove the skin and slice thinly. Sprinkle with lemon juice. Serve pancakes warm, topped with chicken, avocado and a spoonful of mayonnaise and sprinkle with bacon, black pepper and parsley.

Specialty

I really enjoyed putting this next selection of recipes together as I love researching dishes from around the world. In this chapter you will find the fruits of my labors, and proof that pancakes, crepes and waffles are truly a global phenomenon. With subtle changes of ingredients, such as using different flours, adding melted butter and eggs or using different cooking methods like deep-frying and baking, cooks the world over have developed their own variations on the basic batter.

I have included recipes from France as it seems that the French are real masters of batter-making: a deliciously rich cherry batter pudding called Clafoutis and the bistro classic, Crepes suzette – melt-in-the-mouth buttery crepes with the zest and freshness of orange – to name just two.

Going further afield, there are *dosas* from India made with lentil flour, *injera* from Ethiopia, a type of flat bread pancake, and deep-fried pancake rolls from China, stuffed full with tasty shredded vegetables. These recipes require a little more preparation but they are all worth the extra effort required in taste alone!

Russian blinis

Yeasty

Russia's traditional pancakes are made from a yeast batter. They make great canapés, topped with smoked salmon and black lumpfish roe as an inexpensive alternative to caviar.

Makes about 20

1½ cups (180g) **buckwheat flour**
2 tsp **fast-acting dried yeast**
½ tsp **salt**
1 tsp **extra-fine sugar**
2 **eggs**, separated
¾ cup (180ml) **milk**
¼ stick (30g) **unsalted butter**, melted
1¼ cups (300g) **sour cream or crème fraîche**
5oz (150g) **smoked salmon**, finely sliced
3 Tbsp **black lumpfish roe**
Fresh dill, to garnish

Put the flour in a bowl and stir in the yeast, salt and sugar. Make a well in the center and add the egg yolks and milk and gradually whisk to form a smooth, thick batter. Set aside in a warm place for about 1 hour, until doubled in size.

Whisk the egg whites until stiff and carefully fold into the batter. Heat a frying pan until hot and brush with melted butter. Using a dessertspoon, drop spoonfuls of batter on to the pan about 2in (5cm) in diameter and ½in (1cm) thick. Cook over moderate heat for about 1½ minutes on each side until golden.

Turn out onto a wire rack lined with a clean tea towel and baking parchment. Fold the parchment and tea towel over the blinis to keep them warm. Continue to make about 20 blinis, brushing the pan with melted butter as necessary. To serve, top each blini with a little sour cream, a few slices of smoked salmon and a little lumpfish roe. Serve warm, garnished with a small sprig of fresh dill.

Russian blinis

Chinese vegetable pancake rolls

Oriental

These are more like thin omelettes than other pancakes.

Makes 6

½ cup (60g) **plain flour**
¼ cup (60g) **cornstarch**
1 pinch **salt**
3 **eggs,** beaten
2 tsp **sesame oil**
4 tsp **vegetable oil plus extra for deep-frying**
4 **spring onions,** trimmed and sliced
½ cup (125g) **grated carrot**
½ cup (125g) **beansprouts**
1 **clove garlic,** finely chopped
½-in (1-cm) **piece fresh ginger,** peeled and finely chopped
1 tsp **soy sauce**
2 tsp **sweet chilli sauce**

Sift the flour and cornstarch and salt into a bowl and make a well in the center. Add the beaten eggs, 4 Tbsp cold water and the sesame oil and gradually work into the flour to form a smooth batter. Stand for 15 minutes then re-whisk.

Heat a medium frying pan – 8in (20cm) base diameter – until hot and brush lightly with oil. Pour in about ¼ cup (50ml) batter and tilt to cover the base of the pan. Cook over moderate heat, on one side only, for about 2 minutes until set. Make five further pancakes and cover to keep moist until ready to serve.

Heat 2 tsp oil in a wok or large frying pan and stir-fry the vegetables for 1 minute. Add the remaining ingredients, except the oil for deep-frying, and cook for a further minute. Drain well.

Heat the oil for deep-frying to 400°F/200°C. Spoon the vegetables onto the uncooked side of the pancakes. Fold up the ends and the sides, and seal with cocktail sticks. Deep-fry for about 3 minutes, turning, until crisp and brown. Drain, remove cocktail sticks and serve warm with sweet chilli sauce.

French galettes

Continental

These crepes are originally from the French region of Brittany.

Makes 8

¾ cup (180ml) **light beer or lager**
1 cup (125g) **plain flour**
1 cup (125g) **buckwheat flour**
½ tsp **salt**
1 Tbsp **vegetable oil**
1 **egg**
Scant ½ cup (100ml) **milk**
¾ stick (90g) **unsalted butter,** melted
1 **large onion,** finely sliced
7oz (200g) **soft-rind French cheese e.g. Brie,** cut into small pieces
7oz (200g) **lean ham,** cut into thin strips

Mix the beer or lager with an equal quantity of cold water. Sift the flours and salt into a bowl. Make a well in the center and add the oil and egg, whisk gently to form a smooth, thick batter. Leave to stand for 30 minutes. Stir the batter and add sufficient milk to give it the consistency of light cream.

Heat a large frying pan – about 9½in (24cm) base diameter – and brush with a little butter. Ladle in about 3fl oz (90ml) batter to cover the base of the pan. Cook over moderate heat for about 1½ minutes, then turn over and cook for a further minute.

Turn out onto a wire rack lined with a clean tea towel and baking parchment. Cover to keep warm. Make a further seven galettes, brushing the pan with melted butter as necessary.

Heat 1 Tbsp melted butter in a frying pan and gently fry the onion for about 8 minutes until soft and golden. To serve, brush the galettes with the remaining melted butter and sprinkle each with onion, cheese and ham. Roll up tightly.

Injera with lamb, beans and spinach

Injera with lamb, beans and spinach
Spongy

I first tasted this interesting bread/pancake in an Ethiopian restaurant and found its sour taste strangely addictive. The idea is to break bits off and use it to scoop up your stew as you eat it. *Injera* is made from a grain called teff, a type of millet available from specialist food suppliers.

Serves 4

1⅔ cups (225g) **whole-wheat, plain or teff flour**
1lb (500g) **lean lamb fillet,** cut into thin slices
2 Tbsp **olive oil**
½–1 tsp **hot chilli powder**
Salt and freshly ground black pepper
1 cup (180g) **thin green beans,** topped and tailed
¼ stick (30g) **butter**
2 **cloves garlic,** finely chopped
5 cups (250g) **baby spinach,** leaves trimmed
1 tsp **ground cumin**

Put the flour in a mixing bowl and gradually whisk in 2¼ cups (475ml) water to make a smooth batter the consistency of heavy cream. Cover with a clean cloth and leave in a cool place for 3–5 days to ferment, until bubbling and slightly sour in smell. If you are using teff flour, the fermentation will occur more quickly.

When the batter is ready to cook, prepare the lamb. Place the lamb in a bowl and mix in half the olive oil, chilli powder to taste and plenty of seasoning. Cover and chill for about 1 hour. Bring a small saucepan of water to a boil and lightly cook the beans for about 3 minutes. Drain and rinse in cold water to cool. Set aside.
(Recipe continues on page 92.)

Injera with lamb, beans and spinach
continued

Heat a large non-stick frying pan – about 9½in (24cm) base diameter – to a medium temperature. Take care with the temperature: if the pan is too hot the pancake will be too crisp, and if it is too cold it will stick. When a drop of water sizzles and bounces off the surface, the pan is ready to use. Pour about ½ cup (100ml) batter into the pan in circles from the outside towards the center and swirl the pan to coat the base evenly. Cook for about 5 minutes until bubbles appear all over the surface and it looks dry. Cook on one side only. Slide the cooked *injera* onto a wire rack to cool, then stack between layers of baking parchment. You should make about six in total.

Preheat the broiler to a medium-to-hot setting. Thread the lamb on to eight skewers and place on the broiler rack. Cook for about 3 minutes on each side. Remove the lamb from the skewers, and keep warm.

In a large frying pan, heat the remaining oil with the butter until melted together and gently fry the garlic for 3 minutes until softened. Add the green beans with the spinach and ground cumin. Cook, stirring, for about 5 minutes until the spinach has wilted and the beans are tender. To serve, place the *injera* overlapping on a large, warmed serving platter and spoon over the lamb, bean and spinach mixtures. To eat, break off pieces of *injera*, wrap up the food and eat with your fingers.

■ *Quick* injera *recipe:*
2 cups (250g) self-rising flour
½ cup (60g) whole-wheat flour
½ tsp salt
¼ tsp baking powder
2¼ cups (500ml) club soda

Mix the flours, salt and baking powder in a large mixing bowl and gradually whisk in the soda water to make a smooth batter the consistency of heavy cream. Cook as above to make about eight injera.

Crepes suzette
Decadent

The French love their crepes, and this is a classic way to serve them. Submerged in a buttery orange syrup, these crepes will look stunning when flambéed in front of your guests.

Serves 6

1 quantity **Basic crepe batter (see page 24), sweetened**
4 Tbsp + 1 tsp **orange liqueur e.g. Grand Marnier or Cointreau**
6 Tbsp + 1 tsp **freshly squeezed orange juice**
1 stick (125g) **unsalted butter**
Generous ½ cup (125g) **extra-fine sugar**
1 tsp **finely grated orange rind**
2 **sweet oranges,** peeled and divided into segments
1 quantity **Sweet citrus butter (see page 163) (optional)**

Make up the sweetened crepe batter (see page 24), adding 1 tsp orange liqueur and 1 tsp orange juice. Cook the crepes and keep them warm.

Put the butter and sugar in a saucepan and heat gently until the sugar melts. Stir in the remaining orange juice, 2 Tbsp orange liqueur and the orange rind. Bring to a boil and simmer for about 4 minutes until syrupy. Transfer the syrup to a large frying pan.

Fold the crepes in half and then in half again. Arrange them in the syrup and top with orange segments. Heat gently for about 2 minutes. Warm the remaining 2 Tbsp of orange liqueur and pour over the top of the crepes. Carefully light with a taper or long match and serve while flaming. Serve with Sweet citrus butter, if liked.

Dosas with spicy potato sauce
Exotic

These are a popular breakfast food from southern India.

Serves 4

1¼ cups (150g) **finely ground Basmati rice flour and** 1¼ cups
   (150g) **finely ground red lentil or gram (chickpea) flour,**
   soaked and chilled overnight in 1¼ cups (300ml) **buttermilk**
4 tsp **vegetable oil**
1 **medium onion,** chopped
1 tsp **cumin seeds,** lightly crushed
1 tsp **coriander seeds,** lightly crushed
1lb (500g) **potatoes,** peeled and cut into small pieces
1¼ cups (300ml) **vegetable stock**
1 **beef tomato,** chopped
1 **bay leaf**
Salt and freshly ground black pepper
1 quantity **Mango, red onion and tomato salsa (see page 170)**

Heat 2 tsp oil in a saucepan and gently fry the onion and seeds
for 5 minutes until softened. Stir in the potato and cook for
1 minute. Add the stock, tomato and bay leaf. Bring to a boil and
simmer gently, uncovered, for about 30 minutes until tender.
Season well and discard the bay leaf. Keep warm.

For the batter, gradually whisk about ½ cup (100ml) water and
1 tsp salt into the rice and lentil mixture to form a thick dropping
consistency. Heat a small crepe pan – about 6in (15cm) base
diameter – and brush lightly with oil. Ladle in about 3½ Tbsp
batter, spread to an even thickness and cook over moderate heat
for about 1½ minutes on both sides. Make a further 11 *dosas* and
cover to keep warm until ready to serve. Serve the *dosas* while
still warm, topped with the spicy potato sauce and salsa.

Dosas with spicy potato sauce

Spiced chickpea pancakes with eggplant and coconut curry

Inspirational

This dish is inspired by the flavors of Malaysian cuisine.

Serves 4

Salt
2 **eggplants,** cubed
1½ cups (180g) **chickpea, gram or besan flour**
1 tsp **ground coriander**
1 tsp **ground cumin**
2 **dried bird's eye chillies,** finely chopped
½ tsp **salt**
7 Tbsp **vegetable oil**
1 **large onion,** finely sliced
2 **cloves garlic,** crushed
1-in (2.5-cm) **piece fresh ginger,** peeled and chopped
2 **kaffir lime leaves**
1¼ cups (300ml) **coconut milk**
4 Tbsp **finely chopped fresh cilantro**

Salt the eggplant and set aside for 30 minutes. Rinse and dry with paper towel.

Sift the flour into a bowl and make a well in the center. Add the spices, chillies, and ½ tsp salt, and make a well in the center. Whisk in 3 Tbsp oil and 1¼ cups (300ml) warm water to make a smooth batter.

Heat a crepe pan – about 6in (15cm) base diameter – over moderate heat and brush lightly with oil. Ladle in about 3 Tbsp batter and cook over moderate heat for about 1½ minutes until lightly golden, turn over and cook for a further 1½ minutes. Make a further 11 pancakes and cover to keep warm.

Heat the remaining oil in a large saucepan and gently stir-fry the onion, garlic, ginger and lime leaves for about 2 minutes. Add the eggplant and cook, stirring, for 10 minutes until softened. Pour in the coconut milk and simmer gently for 5 minutes. Discard the lime leaves. Stir in the finely chopped cilantro and serve with the pancakes.

Blintzes

Indulgent

A Jewish-American specialty served with a range of toppings, from simple sugar to fresh-fruit sauces. Try serving them with rich Butterscotch sauce (see page 166), or a refreshing fruit coulis (see page 165).

Makes 12

1 quantity **Basic crepe batter (see page 24),** sweetened
1 cup (250g) **cottage cheese**
Scant ½ cup (90g) **full-fat cream cheese**
¼ cup (60g) **extra-fine sugar**
½ tsp **vanilla extract**
¼ stick (30g) **unsalted butter**
1 quantity **Fresh mixed berry or Tropical fruit coulis (see page 165), or Butterscotch sauce (see page 166)**

Prepare and cook the batter (see page 24), and set aside until required. In a bowl, beat together the cheeses, sugar and vanilla extract.

Divide the cheese mixture into 12 equal portions and spread a portion onto the center of each crepe. Fold two sides of the crepe over the filling, towards the middle, and then roll up from one end and secure with large toothpicks.

Melt the butter in a large frying pan until bubbling, then gently fry the rolled pancakes for about 5 minutes, turning, until browned all over. Take care not to over-heat the butter as it may burn. Drain, discard the large toothpicks and serve warm with the coulis or Butterscotch sauce to pour over.

Cherry clafoutis

Sweet and juicy

A much-loved, irresistibly rich French pudding, half pancake batter and half custard. It is best made with fresh cherries when they are in season.

Serves 6

⅔ cup (90g) **plain flour**
3 Tbsp **extra-fine sugar**
½ tsp **salt**
4 **eggs,** beaten
1¼ cups (300ml) **milk**
⅔ cup (150ml) **light cream**
1 tsp **vanilla extract**
1 Tbsp (15g) **unsalted butter,** softened
3 cups (500g) **fresh cherries,** pitted
Confectioners sugar, to dust

To serve:
Light cream (optional)

Preheat the oven to 375°F/190°C. Sift the flour, sugar and salt into a bowl and make a well in the center. Add the eggs and pour in the milk and cream. Gradually work the flour into the eggs and milk and whisk to form a smooth, thick batter. Stir in the vanilla extract.

Grease a 10-in (25-cm) round or shaped baking dish with the butter, add the cherries and pour the batter over them. Place the dish on a baking sheet and bake in the oven for about 45 minutes, until risen and golden – the middle should be just set. Serve warm, dusted with confectioners sugar and accompanied with light cream if liked.

Cherry clafoutis

Sour cream waffles

Creamy sweet

A traditional dish from Norway called *Fløtevafler*, these were traditionally cooked on special cast-iron waffle irons made by the local blacksmith and embossed with individual patterns. Traditionally served with lingonberry or other tart jam.

Makes about 15

5 **eggs**
Generous ½ cup (125g) **extra-fine sugar**
1 cup (125g) **plain flour**
½ tsp **ground cardamom**
¾ cup (180ml) **sour cream**
½ stick (60g) **unsalted butter,** melted, plus extra to serve
Sour cherry jam, to serve

In a large bowl, beat together the eggs and sugar until thick and pale. Sieve in the flour and cardamom, and carefully fold into the whisked eggs together with the sour cream until well incorporated. Gently stir in ½ stick (60g) melted butter and set aside for 10 minutes.

Prepare the waffle irons or waffle machine as directed. Ladle about 3 Tbsp batter over each plate, ensuring that the moulded surface of the lower plate is covered sufficiently. Close the irons and cook until the waffles are just brown on the outside, about 3 minutes. Note: these waffles will be softer than those made with a more traditional batter.

When the waffles are ready, remove them with a two-pronged fork or a skewer, taking care not to scratch the non-stick coating. Place on a wire rack lined with a clean tea towel and baking parchment. Fold the paper and towel over the waffle to keep it moist. Continue to make about 15 waffles, stacking the cooked waffles between sheets of parchment until you are ready to serve. Serve warm, drizzled with melted butter and sour-cherry jam.

Sour cream waffles

Desserts

If you're anything like me, you will always want to know what's for dessert so you know how much room to leave! And, if pancakes are on the menu, then I make sure I leave plenty of space.

Here's a mouthwatering selection assembled in this chapter, from recipes for a sophisticated dinner party, to simple, yet tempting, everyday puddings.

For something quick to go with a mid-week supper, why not try Mini chocolate chip pancakes – they look fantastic piled in a tower, drizzled with chocolate sauce, or Rocky road waffles, topped off with mini marshmallows and ice cream. If it's a special occasion, Mocha crepes are definitely worth a try served with coffee ice cream, or tropical tasting Toasted coconut crepes filled with a juicy fruit cocktail. Both will impress your guests and tickle the taste buds.

By the way, if you've ever thought that pancakes are off the menu because you're watching your weight, then think again. I've included a recipe for low-fat Lace crepes, filled with a fresh green fruit salad.

Apple and pecan pancakes

Saucy

No one will be able to resist these soft, spongy pancakes flavored with sweet applesauce and a pinch of cinnamon.

Serves 4

1 cup (125g) **plain flour**
2 tsp **baking powder**
½ tsp **baking soda**
1 tsp **ground cinnamon**
1 Tbsp **extra-fine sugar**
½ tsp **salt**
2 **eggs**, separated
1 cup (250ml) **buttermilk**
4 Tbsp **applesauce**
¼ stick (30g) **unsalted butter**
½ cup (60g) **pecan halves,**
   roughly chopped
8 Tbsp **maple syrup**

Sift the flour, baking powder, soda, cinnamon, sugar and salt into a bowl and make a well in the center. Add the egg yolks, pour in the buttermilk and gradually work into the flour using a whisk. Beat until thick and smooth, but don't over-mix.

Whisk the egg whites until stiff and, using a large metal spoon, fold carefully into the batter together with the applesauce.

Heat a little butter in a large frying pan until bubbling, tilting the pan to coat the sides. Ladle large spoonfuls, about ¼ cup (50ml), of batter to form pancakes about 4in (10cm) in diameter. Cook over moderate heat for 2 minutes until bubbles appear on the surface. Turn the pancakes and cook for a further 2 minutes until golden. The pancake should puff up and thicken in depth.

Turn the pancakes out onto a wire rack lined with a clean tea towel and baking parchment. Cover. Repeat the process to make 12 pancakes in total, re-buttering the pan as necessary, and stacking the cooked pancakes between sheets of parchment. Serve layered with chopped pecans and maple syrup.

Mixed berry soufflé pancakes

Light and airy

To enjoy these at their best you have to serve them as they come out of the oven, before the air escapes.

Serves 4

1 quantity **Basic pancake batter (see page 22),** sweetened
Scant ½ stick (45g) **unsalted butter**
¼ cup (30g) **plain flour**
Scant 1 cup (210ml) **milk**
¼ cup (60g) **extra-fine sugar**
2 **large eggs,** separated
1 **large egg yolk**
1 tsp **vanilla extract**
Confectioners sugar, to dust
1 quantity **Fresh mixed berry coulis (see page 165)**

Prepare the pancake batter and cook to make eight pancakes. Set aside while preparing the soufflé.

In a saucepan, melt the butter and add the flour. Remove from the heat and gradually stir in the milk. Return to the heat and cook, stirring, until the mixture boils and thickens. Cook for a further minute. Remove from the heat and stir in the sugar and the three egg yolks. Transfer to a bowl and cover the surface with damp greaseproof paper. Leave to cool for 20 minutes.

Preheat the oven to 425°F/220°C. Whisk the egg whites until stiff and carefully fold into the prepared soufflé mixture together with the vanilla extract. Place the pancakes on a large baking sheet lined with baking parchment and spoon over one-eighth of the soufflé mixture onto half of each pancake. Fold the pancakes over to enclose the soufflé mixture.

Bake in the oven for about 10 minutes until golden and lightly set. Serve immediately, dusted with sugar and the fruit coulis poured over the top.

Rocky road waffle stack

Fun

This recipe has a real party feel to it. Just how high you stack the waffles is up to you – and gravity! You can improvise using your own favorite sprinkles and sauces.

Serves 6

1 quantity **Basic waffle batter (see page 25),** sweetened
1-quart (1-L) **tub of your favorite ice cream**
2 cups (100g) **mini marshmallows**
1 quantity **Chocolate sauce (see page 167)**
Scant 1 cup (100g) **chopped mixed nuts**

Prepare the waffle batter, then cook the waffles and keep warm until you are ready to serve.

Simply layer up the waffles on a serving plate and top with a scoop of ice cream, a few marshmallows, a drizzle of chocolate sauce and some chopped nuts. Serve immediately.

■ *You can create waffle stacks with a variety of themes, inspired by your favorite flavors. A few good combinations are listed below:*
– Strawberry ice cream, Fresh mixed berry coulis (see page 165) and fresh strawberries
– Mango sorbet, Tropical fruit coulis (see page 165), freshly chopped banana and kiwi fruit
– Coffee ice cream, Butterscotch sauce (see page 166) and finely chopped toasted walnuts

Rocky road waffle stack

Toasted coconut crepes

Tropical

The flavors of summer are wrapped up in these fruity bundles.

Serves 6

1½ cups (180g) **plain flour**
Pinch **salt**
2 **eggs**
14-fl oz (400-ml) **can light coconut milk**
¾ cup (180g) **granulated sugar**
4 **limes**
Melted butter, for brushing
¾ cup (45g) **shredded coconut**
1 Tbsp **vegetable oil**
2 **large ripe papayas,** peeled, pitted and sliced
6 **scoops coconut ice cream**
Lime zest, to decorate

Sift the flour and salt into a bowl and make a well in the center. Add the eggs, coconut milk and 1¼ cups (300ml) cold water, then whisk until smooth. Cover and stand for 30 minutes.

Meanwhile make the lime syrup. Put the sugar in a saucepan with ¾ cup (180ml) water, and heat, stirring, until dissolved. Pare the rind from two of the limes and extract the juice from all the limes. Add to the pan. Bring to a boil and boil rapidly for 10 minutes. Remove from the heat and set aside. Remove and discard the lime rind.

Whisk the batter again. Heat a crepe pan – about 6in (15cm) base diameter – and brush with a little melted butter. Pour about 2fl oz (50ml) batter into the pan, tilting the pan to coat the base, and quickly sprinkle over a little coconut before the crepe sets. Place over moderate heat and cook for about 1 minute. Turn over and cook for another minute. Make a further 11 crepes and cover to keep moist.

Fill each crepe with a few pieces of papaya and roll up. Top with ice cream, lime zest and lime syrup.

Toasted coconut crepes

Banana and butterscotch waffles

Banana and butterscotch waffles

Kids' favorite

This recipe would be great to serve up at a children's party. You could make the waffles and butterscotch sauce in advance, then assemble the waffles just before serving.

Serves 6

½ quantity **Basic waffle mixture (see page 25)**, sweetened, made up using **banana-flavored milk**
3 **large bananas**
6 **scoops vanilla ice cream**
1 quantity **Butterscotch sauce (see page 166)**

Prepare the half quantity of sweetened waffle batter, replacing the milk with an equal quantity of banana-flavored milk. Cook and keep warm until you are ready to serve.

Just before serving, peel and thinly slice the bananas. Place a waffle on each serving plate and top with banana slices, a scoop of ice cream and some butterscotch sauce. Serve immediately.

Apple strudel pancakes
Sugar and spice

Rich and delicious, serve these fruity pancakes with yogurt, ice cream or Sweet vanilla custard sauce (see page 168).

Serves 4

½ quantity **Basic pancake batter (see page 22),** sweetened
½ stick (60g) **unsalted butter**
Scant ½ cup (60g) **light brown sugar**
3 **dessert apples,** peeled, cored and thinly sliced
Finely grated rind and juice of 1 **lemon**
⅓ cup (60g) **sultanas or golden raisins**
⅓ cup (60g) **glacé cherries,** sliced
½ tsp **ground nutmeg**
Confectioners sugar, to dust

Prepare the pancake batter and cook to make four pancakes. Set aside to keep warm while you prepare the filling.

Melt the butter and sugar in a frying pan until the sugar dissolves. Toss the apples in the lemon rind and juice, add to the pan and cook, stirring, for about 5 minutes. Stir in the sultanas, cherries and nutmeg and continue to cook for a further 2 minutes.

To serve, spoon some filling into the center of each pancake. Fold two sides into the center to overlap the filling slightly. Bring the remaining sides over and flip over to form a square-shaped parcel. Cut in half diagonally and serve dusted with confectioners sugar.

Apple strudel pancakes

Pumpkin pie plate pancakes

Golden

Thick, richly fruited pancakes, ideal to serve at a Halloween party. Can be served cold, spread with butter.

Serves 4

1 cup (125g) **plain flour**
2 tsp **baking powder**
½ tsp **baking soda**
1 tsp **mixed spice**
1 Tbsp **extra-fine sugar**
½ tsp **salt**
2 **eggs**, separated
1 cup (250ml) **buttermilk**
4 Tbsp **pumpkin purée**
⅓ cup (60g) **sultanas or golden raisins**
Unsalted butter, for cooking
Light cream
Maple syrup

Sift the flour, baking powder, soda, mixed spice, sugar and salt into a bowl and make a well in the center. Add the egg yolks, pour in the buttermilk and gradually work into the flour using a whisk. Beat until thick and smooth but don't over-mix.

Whisk the egg whites until stiff and, using a large metal spoon, carefully fold into the batter together with the pumpkin purée and sultanas.

Heat a little butter in a crepe pan – about 6in (15cm) base diameter – until bubbling, tilting the pan to coat the sides. Ladle a quarter of the batter into the pan, tilting the pan to coat the base evenly. Cook over low-to-moderate heat for about 2½ minutes until bubbles appear on the surface. Turn the pancake and cook for a further 2½ minutes until richly golden. The pancake should puff up and thicken in depth.

Turn the pancake out onto a wire rack lined with a clean tea towel and baking parchment. Cover to keep moist. Repeat this process, making four pancakes in total to use up all the batter. Serve warm drizzled with light cream and maple syrup.

Brown sugar and ginger waffles

Syrupy

For grown-ups you could replace some of the milk in the batter with dark rum for extra flavor and, for an added kick, drizzle a little rum over the warm pineapple before serving.

Serves 6

1 quantity **Basic waffle batter (see page 25),** unsweetened
¾ cup (90g) **dark brown sugar**
1 tsp **ground ginger**
1 **ripe medium pineapple,** peeled and cut into 12 slices
Scant ½ stick (45g) **unsalted butter,** melted

To serve:
Whipped cream or yogurt

Prepare the waffle batter (see page 25), replacing the extra-fine sugar with an equal quantity of dark brown sugar. Add the ground ginger to the batter. Cook the waffles and keep warm until required.

Preheat the broiler to a hot setting and line the broiler rack with foil. Arrange the pineapple slices on top and brush with a little butter. Cook for 2 minutes. Turn over, brush with any remaining butter and sprinkle over the remaining dark brown sugar. Continue to cook for about 2 minutes until the sugar bubbles.

To serve, arrange the waffles on serving plates and top with pineapple. Serve with whipped cream or yogurt.

Almond waffles with cherry compôte

Juicy

When cherries are in season, and at their plumpest and juiciest, there is no fruit to rival them. They require only minimal cooking so they retain some texture.

Serves 6

1 cup (200g) **extra-fine sugar**
3¾ cups (625g) **fresh cherries,** washed and pitted
1 **vanilla pod**
1 quantity **Basic waffle batter (see page 25),** sweetened
½ cup (60g) **ground almonds**
1 tsp **almond extract**
4 **scoops vanilla ice cream**
Generous ¼ cup (45g) **toasted flaked almonds**

Put the sugar in a saucepan with 1 scant cup (210ml) water, and heat, stirring, until dissolved. Bring to a boil and add the cherries. Simmer gently for about 5 minutes, stirring occasionally until tender.

Carefully split the vanilla pod down the center, and pry open the sides of the pod. Add to the cherries and syrup, and set aside to cool. Discard the vanilla pod before serving.

Prepare the waffle batter (see page 25), replacing half of the flour with the ground almonds and adding the almond extract to the batter. Cook the waffles and keep them warm until you are ready to serve.

To serve, arrange the waffles on serving plates and spoon over the cherry compôte. Top with a scoop of ice cream and a few flaked almonds.

Almond waffles with cherry compôte

Vanilla crepes with autumn fruits

Vanilla crepes with autumn fruits
Autumnal

Blackberries are one of my favorite fruits and I'm lucky enough to have plenty of hedgerows nearby to supply them from the wild. Wash them well if you've picked them from a hedgerow and avoid areas where crops have been sprayed.

Serves 4

1 quantity **Basic crepe batter (see page 24)**, sweetened
1 tsp **vanilla extract**
½ stick (60g) **unsalted butter**
Scant ½ cup (60g) **light brown sugar**
4 **sweet apples,** peeled, cored and cut into thick slices
1 **cinnamon stick,** broken
Scant 1 cup (250g) **blackberries,** defrosted if frozen
⅔ cup (150ml) **unsweetened apple juice**

To serve:
1 quantity **Sweet spiced butter (see page 163)**

Prepare the crepe batter (see page 24), adding the vanilla extract to the batter. Cook the crepes and keep warm until you are ready to serve.

Melt the butter and sugar in a frying pan until the sugar dissolves. Add the apples and cinnamon stick to the pan and cook, stirring, for about 5 minutes. Gently stir in the blackberries and pour over the apple juice. Bring to a boil and simmer for about 5 minutes until just tender. Discard the cinnamon stick.

To serve, carefully fill the crepes with the apples and blackberries and fold them over. Serve dotted with the Sweet spiced butter.

Mini chocolate chip pancakes

Luscious

These pancakes are similar to "drop scones." Serve hot or cold.

Serves 4

1 cup (125g) **plain flour**
2 tsp **baking powder**
½ tsp **baking soda**
1 Tbsp **extra-fine sugar**
½ tsp **salt**
2 **eggs**, separated
1 cup (250ml) **buttermilk**
3½oz (100g) **plain chocolate chips**
¼ stick (30g) **unsalted butter**
⅔ cup (180g) **strawberries, hulled and sliced**
1 quantity **Chocolate sauce (see page 167)**
4 **scoops vanilla ice cream**

Sift the flour, baking powder, soda, sugar and salt into a bowl and make a well in the center. Add the egg yolks and buttermilk, and gradually work into the flour using a whisk. Beat until thick and smooth but don't over-mix.

Whisk the egg whites until stiff and, using a large metal spoon, carefully fold into the batter with the chocolate chips.

Heat a little butter in a large frying pan until bubbling; tilt the pan to coat the sides. Ladle about 2 Tbsp batter to form a small pancake about 3in (7cm) in diameter. Cook over moderate heat for 1 minute until bubbles appear on the surface. Turn the pancakes and cook for a further minute until golden. The pancake should puff up and thicken in depth.

Turn them out onto a wire rack lined with a clean tea towel. Cover to keep moist. Make 16 pancakes in total, re-buttering the pan as necessary and stacking the cooked pancakes between sheets of parchment.

Layer the chocolate chip pancakes with strawberries and chocolate sauce and serve with a scoop of vanilla ice cream.

Mini chocolate chip pancakes

Lemon meringue waffles

Lemon meringue waffles

Tangy

One of my favorite puddings is lemon meringue pie – I love the contrast between the sharp lemon filling and the sweet marshmallow-like topping. Here I have combined the classic flavors and textures of the pie to make a waffle dessert.

Serves 6

½ quantity **Basic waffle batter (see page 25)**, sweetened
1 tsp **finely grated lemon rind**
6 Tbsp **Greek, or whole-milk, yogurt**
6 Tbsp **lemon curd**
6 **small meringues,** lightly crushed
Mint leaves, to decorate

Prepare the half quantity of waffle batter (see page 25), adding the lemon rind to the batter. Cook the waffles and keep warm until you are ready to serve.

To serve, gently swirl the yogurt and lemon curd together and spoon on top of the waffles. Sprinkle with crushed meringue and decorate with mint leaves.

Deep-fried mincemeat pancake pockets
Christmassy

These crispy parcels make a good alternative to traditional plum pudding. You can prepare them well in advance and fry them just before serving.

Serves 6

1 quantity **Basic crepe batter (see page 24)**, sweetened
6 Tbsp **mincemeat**
1 **dessert apple**, peeled, cored and grated
½ cup (125g) **ricotta cheese**
Oil for deep-frying

To serve:
1 quantity **Sweet vanilla custard sauce (see page 168)**

Prepare and cook the crepe batter (see page 24), and keep warm until required. In a bowl, mix together the mincemeat and grated apple.

Divide the mincemeat mixture between each crepe, placing it in the center of each. Top with a smaller spoonful of ricotta cheese. Fold two sides of the crepe over the filling, towards the middle, and then roll up from one end. Secure with a large toothpick.

Heat the oil for deep-frying to 400°F/200°C and fry the rolled pancakes for about 5 minutes, turning in the oil until browned all over. Drain, discard the toothpicks and serve warm with the custard to pour over.

Crepes with chocolate and bananas

Comforting

Thick chocolate custard and bananas is a pudding loved by children. Here it is used to fill thin coconut-flavored crepes, and the combination is sublime.

Serves 6

1 quantity **Basic sweet white sauce (see page 162)**
2oz (60g) **plain chocolate,** grated
1 quantity **Basic crepe batter (see page 24),** sweetened
10-fl oz (300-ml) **can light coconut milk**
4 **medium bananas**
4 Tbsp **light cream**
Confectioners sugar, to dust

Make up the sweet white sauce (see page 162), adding the grated chocolate at the same time as the vanilla extract. Cover the surface with damp wax paper and set aside to cool. Then cover and chill until required.

Prepare the batter (see page 24), replacing the milk with an equal quantity of coconut milk. Cook the crepes and cover to keep moist until you are ready to serve.

To serve, peel and slice the bananas. Gently whisk the cream into the cooled chocolate sauce and fold the sliced banana into the sauce. Fill and roll the crepes and serve dusted with confectioners sugar.

Coffee crepes with caramel oranges

Sophisticated

There is an interesting contrast of flavors in this dessert: bitter coffee, sharp citrus and sweet creamy cheese. The three flavors marry together very well and are certain to be a talking point.

Serves 6

1 cup (250g) **mascarpone cheese**
Generous ½ cup (125g) + 2 Tbsp **extra-fine sugar**
1 tsp **vanilla extract**
6 **medium oranges**
1 quantity **Basic crepe batter (see page 24), sweetened**
4 Tbsp **cold espresso or strong black coffee**
Orange zest, to decorate

In a bowl, mix the mascarpone cheese with 2 Tbsp sugar and the vanilla extract. Cover and chill until required.

Using a sharp knife, slice the tops and bottoms off the oranges. Slice off the peel taking away as much of the white pith as possible. Cut the oranges into thin slices and place in a shallow bowl. Cover and chill until required.

Prepare the batter (see page 24), replacing 4 Tbsp milk with the cold espresso coffee. Cook the crepes and keep warm until required.

Place the remaining sugar in a small saucepan and add 4 Tbsp water. Heat gently until dissolved and then increase the heat. Bring to a boil and boil for about 4 minutes until golden and caramelized. Remove from the heat and plunge the bottom of the pan into cold water to cease the cooking.

To serve, fill the crepes with a generous spoonful of the mascarpone cheese and top with a few orange slices. Drizzle with caramel and quickly fold up. Serve decorated with orange zest.

Coffee crepes with caramel oranges

Chocolate waffles with pears

Heavenly

There's a hint of aniseed in this recipe, which gives a little extra lift to the pears. Aniseed, or star anise, is an ideal flavoring to use with chocolate as well. Replace with cinnamon if preferred.

Serves 6

4 **ripe pears,** peeled, cored and halved
Juice of 1 **lemon**
1¼ cups (300ml) **unsweetened apple or pear juice**
2 **star anise**
1 quantity **Basic waffle batter (see page 25),** sweetened and made with chocolate-flavored milk

To serve:
1 quantity **Chocolate sauce (see page 167)**
Light cream

Gently toss the pears in the lemon juice and place in a shallow pan with a lid. Pour over the fruit juice and add the star anise. Bring to a boil, cover and simmer gently for about 10 minutes. Remove from the heat and allow the pears to cool in the juice. Discard the star anise.

Prepare the batter (see page 25), replacing the milk with an equal quantity of chocolate-flavored milk. Cook the waffles and cover to keep warm until you are ready to serve.

To serve, place a waffle on each serving plate. Drain the pears and arrange on top of each waffle. Serve with hot chocolate sauce and light cream.

Hazelnut waffles with raspberries

Nutty

Hazelnuts give a sweet, nutty flavor to these waffles. Blueberries also make a good topping and, if you prefer a more intense chocolate flavor, you could serve with Chocolate sauce (see page 167).

Serves 6

1 quantity **Basic waffle batter (see page 25)**, sweetened
½ cup (60g) **toasted ground hazelnuts**
2 tsp **hazelnut syrup**
Generous 1 cup (300g) **raspberries**, defrosted if frozen
1 quantity **Chocolate sauce (see page 167)**, made using **white chocolate** instead of dark chocolate
2 Tbsp **toasted hazelnuts**, chopped
Mint leaves to decorate

Prepare the waffle batter (see page 25), replacing half the flour with the ground hazelnuts and adding the hazelnut syrup to the batter. Cook the waffles and keep warm until you are ready to serve.

To serve, arrange the waffles on serving plates and top with raspberries. Spoon over the warm white chocolate sauce and sprinkle with toasted hazelnuts. Decorate with mint leaves.

Lace crepes with green fruit salad

Lace crepes with green fruit salad

Healthy

Delicate, super-light crepes that melt in the mouth, these are a treat for dieters and can be filled with your favorite combination of fruits. They are best served freshly made while still warm. Using a small pitcher to pour the batter in a thin stream will enable you to achieve a delicate definition.

Serves 4

2 cups (250g) **fresh lychees,** peeled and pitted
¼ **green melon e.g. Galia,** deseeded and chopped
1¼ cups (125g) **seedless green grapes**
2 **kiwi fruit,** peeled and chopped
Finely grated rind and juice of 1 **lime**
2 Tbsp **ginger syrup**
3 **large egg whites,** lightly beaten
4 Tbsp **cornstarch**
8 tsp **skim milk**
1 tsp **vegetable oil**

To serve:
Yogurt

Mix all the fruits together and gently toss in the lime rind, juice and ginger syrup. Cover and chill until required.

Put the egg whites and cornstarch in a mixing bowl and stir in the milk, mixing well to form a smooth paste. Brush a non-stick medium frying pan – about 8in (20cm) base diameter – with a little of the oil and heat until hot. Using a quarter of the batter, pour a thin ring of batter around the outside of the pan and then finely drizzle the batter all over to give a lacy effect. Cook over moderate heat for a few seconds on one side only, until set. Drain on paper towel, layer with baking parchment and keep warm while you make the remaining three crepes.

To serve, place a crepe on each serving plate and top with the mixed fruits. Fold the crepes over and serve accompanied with yogurt.

Deep peach pancake with melba sauce

Luscious

A rich, soft, deep pancake filled with peaches.

Serves 6

1 quantity **Basic crepe batter (see page 24)**, sweetened

4 Tbsp **heavy cream**

1 cup (250g) **raspberries**, defrosted if frozen

4 Tbsp **freshly squeezed orange juice**

1 Tbsp **runny honey**

¼ stick (30g) **unsalted butter**

3 **ripe peaches**, pitted and thickly sliced

3 Tbsp **raw brown sugar**

Prepare the batter (see page 24), replacing 4 Tbsp milk with the cream. Set aside.

To make the Melba sauce, put the raspberries in a blender with the orange juice and honey. Blend until smooth. Push through a nylon sieve to remove seeds. Cover and chill until required.

Melt the butter in a large frying pan – about 9½in (24cm) base diameter – until bubbling and gently fry the peaches for about 1 minute, stirring, to coat in the butter. Pour in the batter and cook over low-to-moderate heat for about 6 minutes until set. Keep the heat quite low to prevent the bottom from over-browning, and lift the edges of the pancake to allow the runny batter from the center to flood underneath and cook.

Carefully loosen the pancake and slide out onto a plate or board. Flip over, back into the pan, and cook the other side for a further 5 minutes.

Preheat the broiler to a hot setting. Turn the pancake back over and sprinkle the top thickly with raw brown sugar. Cook under the broiler for about 3 minutes until puffed, golden and bubbling. Serve cut into slices, with the Melba sauce poured over the top.

Mocha crepes with coffee ice cream

After-dinner choice

Serve these crepes while they are still warm to enjoy a delicious mingling of melting coffee ice cream and chocolate sauce, giving you a ready-made cappuccino on your plate!

Serves 4

1 quantity **Basic crepe batter (see page 24), sweetened**
2 Tbsp (15g) **cocoa powder**
4 Tbsp **cold espresso or strong black coffee**
4 **generous scoops coffee ice cream**
1 quantity **Chocolate sauce (see page 167)**
8 **chocolate coffee beans**
1 tsp **milk chocolate powder**

To serve:
Light cream

Prepare the batter (see page 24), replacing ½oz (15g) of the flour with cocoa powder and 4 Tbsp milk with the cold espresso coffee. Cook the crepes and keep warm until required.

When you are ready to serve, fold the crepes into triangles and arrange three per serving plate. Top with a scoop of ice cream and pour over the chocolate sauce. Decorate with chocolate coffee beans and dust lightly with chocolate powder. Serve immediately with light cream.

Snacks

Sometimes you just want a small, comforting morsel to stop a rumbling tummy or a quick snack to keep you going. This section is where you'll find something to suit.

I enjoy this type of food more than any other, as I like the variety it offers. I'm always eyeing other people's plates in restaurants and demanding a taste from them! In this chapter I've put together lots of ideas to show how pancakes and waffles make the perfect "light bite." Among my favorites are the Pesto pancake crisps which make a tasty alternative to the potato variety. There are Sausage and bacon popovers – perfect for party food – or mini mouthful-sized pancakes called Silver dollars, for those with a sweet tooth.

Waffles can be used as a pizza base and as an alternative to a burger bun, filled with a juicy beef burger and salad; they really are very versatile.

And last, but not least, attempt your own English tea by making and then serving soft, thick and spongy Crumpets, served warm, dripping with butter and lots of jam!

Mini banana and sultana pancakes

Fruity

Perfect for an afternoon snack, served warm and buttered with jam or a spread of your choice.

Makes 16

1 cup (125g) **plain flour**
2 tsp **baking powder**
½ tsp **baking soda**
½ tsp **ground nutmeg**
1 Tbsp **extra-fine sugar**
½ tsp **salt**
2 **eggs,** separated
1 cup (250ml) **buttermilk**
1 **large ripe banana,** mashed
⅓ cup (60g) **sultanas or golden raisins**
¼ stick (30g) **unsalted butter**

Sift the flour, baking powder, soda, nutmeg, sugar and salt into a bowl and make a well in the center. Add the egg yolks, pour in the buttermilk and gradually whisk into the flour. Beat until thick and smooth but don't over-mix.

Whisk the egg whites until stiff and, using a large metal spoon, carefully fold into the batter with the mashed banana and sultanas.

Heat a little butter in a large frying pan until bubbling, tilting the pan to coat the sides. Ladle about 2 Tbsp batter to form a small pancake about 2in (5cm) in diameter. Cook over moderate heat for 1 minute until bubbles appear on the surface. Turn the pancake over and cook for a further minute until golden. The pancake should puff up and thicken in depth.

Turn the pancake out onto a wire rack lined with a clean tea towel and baking parchment. Fold the paper and tea towel over the pancake to keep moist. Repeat the process to use up all the batter and make 16 pancakes in total, re-buttering the pan as necessary and stacking the cooked pancakes between sheets of baking parchment until you are ready to serve them.

Cornmeal and paprika griddle cakes

Smoky

You can replace dairy milk with soy milk in most of the recipes in this book, and in this one it works particularly well as it seems to add to a savory flavor. If you don't want the slight kick provided by the hot smoked paprika, then opt for milder paprika.

Makes 8

⅔ cup (90g) **plain flour**
Scant ½ cup (60g) **fine cornmeal**
2 tsp **baking powder**
½ tsp **salt**
½ tsp **hot smoked paprika**
1 tsp **extra-fine sugar**
1 **egg,** separated
1 cup (250ml) **unsweetened soy milk**
½ stick (60g) **butter or** 4 Tbsp **dairy-free margarine,** melted
1 Tbsp **vegetable oil**

Sift the flour, cornmeal, baking powder, salt, paprika and sugar into a bowl. Make a well in the center and add the egg yolk, soy milk and the melted butter or margarine. Whisk into the dry ingredients to form a thick, smooth batter. Take care not to over-beat. Whisk the egg white until stiff, then carefully fold into the batter. Heat a large frying pan or griddle. Brush with a little oil and ladle over about ⅓ cup (90ml) batter into the pan, leaving space for the griddle cake to expand. Cook for about 2 minutes on each side until golden. Or, you could use a 6-in (15-cm) base diameter crepe pan for a more even finish.

Turn the griddle cake out onto a wire rack lined with a clean tea towel and baking parchment. Fold the paper and towel over the cakes to keep moist. Repeat the process to use up all the batter and make eight griddle cakes in total, re-oiling the pan as necessary and stacking the cooked griddle cakes between sheets of parchment until you are ready to serve.

Crepe and fruit skewers

Fun

Serve these colorful creations as a light dessert or snack –
you could easily take them on a picnic. They are also a good
idea for children's parties and an excellent and fun way for
them to eat more fruit.

Makes 12

½ quantity **Basic crepe batter (see page 24),** sweetened
12 **large strawberries,** hulled and halved
1 **ripe star fruit,** sliced
1 **ripe kiwi fruit,** peeled and cut into 12 wedges
1 **small or "mini" mango,** peeled, pitted and cut into chunks

To serve:
1 quantity **Tropical fruit coulis (see page 165)**
Fruit yogurt

Prepare the batter (see page 24) and cook to make six crepes.
Roll up the crepes and cut into 1-in (2.5-cm) thick slices.

Thread strips of pancake and pieces of fruit on to 12 long
bamboo skewers, cover and chill until required. Serve with the
Tropical fruit coulis and fruit yogurt to dip.

■ *If star fruit are not available, replace with thick slices of crisp apple
or Asian pear.*

Crepe and fruit skewers

Pesto pancake crisps

Salty

These are great to serve at a party with salsas or dips. You can experiment with different flavors in the batter or by adding spices to the finished crisps. For a sweet version, try plain pancake batter crisps served sprinkled with cinnamon and sugar.

Serves 6–8

1 quantity **Basic pancake batter (see page 22)**, unsweetened
4 Tbsp **Pesto sauce (see page 168)**
Oil for deep-frying
Sea salt and freshly ground black pepper
Finely grated Parmesan cheese (optional)

Prepare the pancake batter (see page 22), adding the pesto sauce to the finished batter. Cook as described to make eight pancakes, then set aside on wire racks to cool and dry out slightly. Cut the pancakes into eight equal triangular pieces. Heat the oil for deep-frying to 400°F/200°C and fry the pancake pieces a few at a time, in batches, for about 1 minute, turning in the oil until crisp and golden. Drain on paper towel and keep warm while you fry the other pieces.

When you are ready to serve, sprinkle with sea salt and black pepper and serve warm. Sprinkle with grated Parmesan cheese if liked.

Pesto pancake crisps

Mini pancake hot dogs

Fast food

These are perfect for a barbecue. The thick pancakes make edible holders for all sorts of food and they are easy to eat.

Makes 12

½ cup (60g) **buckwheat flour**
½ cup (60g) **plain flour**
1 **pinch salt**
1 **large egg**
1 stick (125g) **unsalted butter,** melted
Scant 1 cup (210ml) **milk**
2 tsp **sweet prepared mustard**
1½lb (750g) **onions,** peeled and thinly sliced
Freshly ground black pepper
12 **good-quality pork sausages**

Sift the flours and salt into a bowl. Make a well in the center and add the egg, ¼ stick (30g) butter, milk and mustard and whisk to form a smooth batter. Set aside for 30 minutes.

Heat ½ stick (60g) butter in a frying pan and cook the onions over moderate heat, stirring occasionally, for about 25 minutes until soft and golden. Season lightly and keep warm.

Preheat the broiler to a medium-to-high setting. Place the sausages on the broiler rack and cook, turning occasionally, for about 25 minutes until cooked through. They take about 20 minutes on the grill.

Cook the batter as per instructions for a Basic crepe (see page 24). Turn out onto a wire rack lined with a clean tea towel and baking parchment. Cover to keep moist. Make a further 11 pancakes, brushing the pan with melted butter as necessary and stacking the pancakes between sheets of parchment.

To serve, place a sausage in the center of each pancake and top with fried onions.

Mini whole-wheat pancake wraps

Wholesome

We're all familiar with tortilla wraps – a variation on a simple sandwich – and this recipe is a new take, using pancakes instead. You can fill them with just about anything, although drier fillings work best as they won't make the pancake soggy.

Makes 8

½ quantity **Basic pancake batter (see page 22),** unsweetened and made with whole-wheat flour
14-oz (400-g) **can tuna in brine,** drained
4 Tbsp **reduced-fat mayonnaise**
4 **spring onions,** trimmed and finely chopped
Salt and freshly ground black pepper
2 **small heads of Boston lettuce,** trimmed and ripped into small pieces
¼ **cucumber,** cut into thin strips
1 **medium carrot,** peeled and cut into thin strips

Prepare the pancake batter (see page 22), using whole-wheat flour instead of white flour. Cook the batter in a crepe pan – about 6in (15cm) base diameter – using about 2 Tbsp batter to make eight pancakes. Set aside to cool.

For the filling, flake the tuna and mix in the mayonnaise and chopped spring onions. Season lightly. Cover and chill until required.

When you are ready to serve, line each pancake with a little lettuce, cucumber, carrot and tuna mixture. Fold both sides into the center to slightly overlap and make a cone shape, then tuck the end underneath. Take care not to over-fill or the wraps will be difficult to roll and messy to eat. You can serve any leftover filling as a salad on the side.

Chickpea and sweetcorn cheese cakes

Chickpea and sweetcorn cheese cakes

Cheesy

Probably one of my favorite recipes in the whole book. These are great served with soup, as an accompaniment to stews or simply buttered as a snack.

Makes 8

⅔ cup (90g) **chickpea, gram or besan flour**
½ cup (60g) **fine cornmeal**
2 tsp **baking powder**
½ tsp **salt**
1 tsp **extra-fine sugar**
2 Tbsp (30g) **finely grated fresh Parmesan cheese**
1 **egg,** separated
½ cup (60g) **sweetcorn kernels**
1 cup (250ml) **milk**
½ stick (60g) **butter,** melted
1 Tbsp **vegetable oil**
Smoked paprika

Sift the flour, cornmeal, baking powder, salt and sugar into a bowl. Stir in the Parmesan. Make a well in the center and add the egg yolk, sweetcorn, milk and melted butter. Whisk into the dry ingredients to form a thick, smooth batter. Take care not to over-beat. Whisk the egg white until stiff, then carefully fold into the batter.

Heat a large frying pan or griddle until hot. Brush with a little oil and pour about ⅓ cup (90ml) of batter into the center of the pan. Cook over low-to-moderate heat for about 2 minutes on each side until golden. Alternatively, cook in a crepe pan – about 6in (15cm) base diameter.

Turn the griddle cake out onto a wire rack lined with a clean tea towel and baking parchment. Cover the cake to keep moist. Make 8 griddle cakes in total, re-oiling the pan as necessary and stacking the cooked griddle cakes between sheets of parchment until you are ready to serve. Best served warm, buttered and sprinkled with smoked paprika.

Sausage and bacon popovers
Savory

A simple idea that is extremely tasty and reminds me of my childhood. These are little hollow quick breads; they are a perfect snacking size and excellent canapés. Try using vegetarian sausages or chopped vegetables for a veggie version.

Makes 12

1¼ cups (150g) **plain flour**
½ tsp **salt**
3 **eggs,** beaten
1 cup (250ml) **milk**
1 tsp **dried mixed herbs**
6 strips **bacon,** halved
   lengthways
24 **cocktail sausages**
3 Tbsp **vegetable oil**

To serve:
Mustard
Tomato ketchup

Sift the flour and salt into a bowl and make a well in the center. Add the eggs, milk and herbs and whisk into the dry ingredients to form a smooth, thin batter. Set aside for 30 minutes.

Cut the bacon strips in half through the middle to create short lengths. Carefully wrap a piece of bacon around each sausage. Cover and chill until you are ready to cook.

Preheat the oven to 375°F/190°C. Spoon ½ tsp oil into each hole of a 12-hole, deep muffin tin and place in the oven for 1 minute until hot. Place 2 sausages side by side in each hole and pour over sufficient batter to come three quarters of the way up each hole. Bake in the oven for about 35 minutes, until risen, golden and crisp. Best served warm, with mustard and tomato ketchup on the side.

Sausage and bacon popovers

Blueberry and cinnamon silver dollars

Moreish

Pancakes are a North American passion, and these little gems, named after the coin they resemble, are very popular.

Makes 24

2 cups (250g) **plain flour**
1 tsp **ground cinnamon**
2 Tbsp **extra-fine sugar**
2 tsp **baking powder**
½ tsp **salt**
4 Tbsp **vegetable oil**
1 **egg**
1 cup (250ml) **milk**
Scant ½ cup (90g)
  blueberries, defrosted if
  frozen
Maple syrup, to serve

Sift the flour, cinnamon, sugar, baking powder and salt into a bowl and make a well in the center. Add 3 Tbsp oil, the egg and milk, and gradually whisk into the dry ingredients to form a smooth, thick batter. Fold in the blueberries. Take care not to over-mix.

Heat a large frying or griddle pan until hot and brush lightly with oil. Ladle about 1 Tbsp batter to form a small pancake about 2in (5cm) in diameter. Cook over moderate heat for about 1½ minutes until bubbles appear on the surface. Slide a palette knife under the pancakes and flip over. Brown the underside of the pancakes for a further minute until golden. The pancake should puff up and thicken in depth.

Turn the pancakes out onto a wire rack lined with a clean tea towel and baking parchment. Fold the paper and towel over the pancakes to keep moist. Repeat the process to use up all the batter and make 24 pancakes in total, re-oiling the pan as necessary and stacking the cooked pancakes between sheets of parchment until you are ready to serve. Best served warm drizzled with maple syrup.

Blueberry and cinnamon silver dollars

Silver dollar marshmallow pancakes
Fun

A variation on the Blueberry and cinnamon silver dollars recipe (see page 148) that will be popular as a sweet party treat. You could serve the pancakes separately with an assortment of spreads and toppings and let your guests make up their own combinations.

Makes 24

2 cups (250g) **plain flour**
2 Tbsp **extra-fine sugar**
2 tsp **baking powder**
½ tsp **salt**
4 Tbsp **vegetable oil**
1 **egg**
1 cup (250ml) **chocolate-flavored milk**
½ cup (90g) **milk chocolate chips**
4 Tbsp **chocolate spread**
24 large **marshmallows**

Make up the batter as for the Blueberry and cinnamon silver dollars (see page 148), omitting the ground cinnamon and replacing the milk with chocolate-flavored milk, and the blueberries with chocolate chips. Cook as described and allow to cool.

To serve, spread the silver dollar pancakes thickly with chocolate spread and top each with a marshmallow.

Raspberry and chocolate popovers

Jammy

My grandmother used to make plain popovers for a simple pudding and she served them with golden syrup poured over. Here I've added a little chocolate and some jam for sweetness. Dark chocolate and cherry jam also make a good combination.

Makes 12

1¼ cups (150g) **plain flour**
½ tsp **salt**
3 **medium eggs,** beaten
1 cup (250ml) **milk**
2 Tbsp **vegetable oil**
12 small squares **white chocolate**
12 tsp **raspberry jam**

Sift the flour and salt into a bowl and make a well in the center. Add the eggs and milk and whisk into the dry ingredients to form a smooth, thin batter. Set aside for 30 minutes.

Preheat the oven to 375°F/190°C. Spoon ½ tsp oil into each hole of a 12-hole, deep muffin tin and place in the oven for 1 minute until hot. Divide the batter between the holes to come about three-quarters of the way up each and bake for about 15 minutes until just starting to rise but still soft in the middle. Gently push a square of chocolate into the center of each and top with a tsp of jam. Bake for a further 10 minutes until risen, golden and crisp. Best served warm.

■ *Remember that jam keeps its heat for quite a while, so take care not to burn yourself if eating right away.*

Toasted pizza waffles

Toasted pizza waffles
Herbed

Because waffles have a pitted surface, it is often difficult to spread some toppings, such as a pizza sauce, evenly over the top. Tiny slices of cherry tomato, however, sit neatly on top and give an excellent sweet and fresh tomato flavor.

Serves 6

1 quantity **Basic waffle batter (see page 25)**, unsweetened
4 Tbsp **Pesto sauce (see page 168)**
5 cups (250g) **vine-ripened cherry tomatoes**, sliced
¼ cup (60g) **pitted black olives in brine**, drained and sliced
7oz (210g) **ball mozzarella cheese**, cut into 12 slices
1 tsp **dried oregano**
Freshly ground black pepper
Fresh basil leaves, to garnish

Make up the batter (see page 25), adding the pesto sauce to the finished batter. Cook as described to make 12 waffles.

Preheat the broiler to a medium-to-hot setting. Line the broiler rack with foil and arrange the waffles on top. Arrange slices of cherry tomato all over the top of the waffles and sprinkle with sliced olives. Arrange two slices of mozzarella cheese on top and sprinkle lightly with oregano and black pepper. Cook under the broiler for about 3 minutes until the cheese has melted. Serve immediately, garnished with a few basil leaves.

Waffle burger

Fast food

These are substantial snacks. For a lighter option halve the batter quantity to make six waffles, and set a burger and the trimmings on top instead of sandwiching with another waffle.

Makes 6

1lb 4oz (625g) **lean ground beef**
1 **medium onion,** finely chopped
3 Tbsp **finely chopped fresh parsley**
1 quantity **Basic waffle batter (see page 25),** unsweetened
2 Tbsp **toasted sesame seeds**
Few **lettuce leaves**
12 **slices ripe tomato**
Few slices **red onion**
Few slices **dill pickle**

To serve:
Sweet mustard
Tomato ketchup

First make the burgers. In a bowl, mix the beef with the chopped onion and parsley. Divide into six equal portions and form into 4-in (10-cm) diameter patties. Cover and chill until ready to cook.

Make up the batter (see page 25), adding the sesame seeds to the finished batter. Cook as described to make 12 waffles.

Preheat the broiler to a medium-to-hot setting. Arrange the burgers on the broiler rack and cook the burgers for about 7 minutes on each side, or until cooked through to your liking. Drain.

To serve, top six waffles with lettuce and tomato and sit a burger on top. Add a few slices of red onion and dill pickle and place another waffle on top. Serve immediately with sweet mustard and tomato ketchup.

Waffle burger

Sweet butterscotch waffle sandwiches

Sweet butterscotch waffle sandwiches

Irresistible

If you have a sweet tooth, then this is the waffle for you!
You can use any flavor of ice cream and sauce you fancy
to make your personalized sweet treat.

Serves 6

1 quantity **Basic waffle batter (see page 25),** sweetened
2 Tbsp **maple syrup**
12 **scoops toffee ice cream**
⅔ cup (180g) **blueberries,** defrosted if frozen
1 quantity **Butterscotch sauce (see page 166)**
1 Tbsp **confectioners sugar**

Make up the batter (see page 25), adding the maple syrup to
the finished batter. Cook as described to make 12 waffles.
Allow to cool.

When you are ready to serve, place six waffles on serving plates
and top each with two scoops of ice cream, a few blueberries
and a generous drizzle of sauce. Top with another waffle and
press down gently to make "sandwiches." Serve immediately,
dusted with confectioners sugar and accompanied with the
remaining butterscotch sauce.

Tea-time crumpets

Spongy

Try your own English afternoon tea, complete with crumpets. Not strictly a pancake, the yeasty batter is cooked in rings on a griddle pan to give thick "cakes," crisp on the outside and spongy soft in the middle.

Makes 10

2 cups (250g) **white bread flour**
½ tsp **salt**
1 Tbsp **extra-fine sugar**
2 tsp **fast-acting dried yeast**
1½ cups (350ml) **milk, lukewarm**
1 Tbsp **vegetable oil**

To serve:
Butter
Jam

Sift the flour, salt and sugar into a bowl and stir in the yeast. Make a well in the center and pour in the milk. Gradually mix into the dry ingredients to form a thick batter. Cover loosely and set aside in a warm place for about 1 hour until the batter is frothy and has doubled in size.

Heat a large frying or griddle pan until hot and brush lightly with oil. Lightly grease four 3½-in (9-cm) diameter metal crumpet rings or plain round cutters and arrange them side by side in the pan. Ladle in sufficient batter to a depth of about ½in (2cm) and cook over low-to-moderate heat for about 8 minutes until risen and the bubbles on the surface burst and set. Take care not to over-brown the undersides. Carefully remove the crumpets from the rings, turn over and cook for another minute to brown the top lightly. Transfer to a wire rack to cool and repeat the process until all the batter is used up – you should be able to make 10 crumpets.

To serve, toast the crumpets lightly and serve spread with butter and jam.

Tea-time crumpets

Ham and cheese pancake rolls

Tasty

When cut in half, these pancakes reveal a tight spiral of pink ham and oozing cheese. They are delicious served with a tangy pickle or chutney to dip into.

Makes 12

1 quantity **Mini pancake batter (see page 142)**
2 tsp **wholegrain mustard**
2 tsp **olive oil**
½ quantity **Basic savory white sauce (see page 162)**, cold
4oz (125g) **Gruyère cheese**, finely grated
Freshly ground black pepper
12 wafer-thin slices **lean ham**

Make up the batter (see page 142), replacing the prepared mustard with wholegrain, and cook to make 12 small pancakes. Allow to cool.

Preheat the oven to 400°F/200°C. Lightly grease a shallow ovenproof dish with the olive oil. Spread each pancake with white sauce, and sprinkle over a little cheese and black pepper. Lay a slice of ham on each. Roll up tightly and place side by side in the dish. Bake for about 15 minutes until hot and melting. Allow to stand for 5 minutes, then slice in half and serve wrapped in wax paper for easier eating.

Ham and cheese pancake rolls

Accompaniments

Basic savory white sauce

Makes approx. 2½ cups (600ml)

½ stick (45g) **butter**
⅓ cup (45g) **plain flour**
2½ cups (600ml) **milk**
Salt and freshly ground black pepper

Melt the butter in a saucepan, add the flour and stir until smooth. Cook gently for
2 minutes, stirring, until bubbling. Remove from the heat and gradually stir in the milk.
Return to a moderate heat and bring to a boil, stirring continuously, and cook gently
for about 3 minutes. Add seasoning to taste and serve.

■ *For a cheese sauce – add 4oz (125g) grated mature Cheddar and ¼ tsp dry mustard powder.*
■ *For a herb sauce – add 4 Tbsp assorted finely chopped herbs, such as parsley, chives or sage.*

Basic sweet white sauce

Makes approx. 2½ cups (600ml)

3 Tbsp **cornstarch**
2½ cups (600ml) **milk**
1 tsp **vanilla extract or almond essence**
2–3 Tbsp **extra-fine sugar**

Blend the cornstarch with 6 Tbsp of the milk to form a smooth paste. Heat the
remaining milk in a large saucepan until boiling and add the paste, stirring continuously.
Bring back to a boil, still stirring, and cook for 2 minutes until thick and glossy. Add the
vanilla extract (or almond essence if preferred) and sugar to taste, and serve.

■ *Flavor with 1 tsp cinnamon; or 2 Tbsp jam; or 2oz (50g) grated plain chocolate; or 2 Tbsp rum.*

Sweet spiced butter

Makes approx. ½ cup (100g)

¾ stick (90g) **unsalted butter, softened**
1 Tbsp **extra-fine sugar**
1 tsp **ground cinnamon**

Combine all three ingredients together in a small bowl until well mixed. Pile onto a double-thick layer of plastic wrap and roll up the butter into a thick roll about 1in (2.5cm) thick. Wrap tightly and chill for at least 30 minutes until you are ready to use it.

■ *To vary the flavor, replace the cinnamon with ground ginger or mixed spice.*

Sweet citrus butter

Makes approx. ½ cup (100g)

¾ stick (90g) **unsalted butter, softened**
1 Tbsp **light brown sugar**
½ tsp **finely grated lemon rind**
½ tsp **finely grated orange rind**

Combine all the ingredients together in a small bowl until well mixed. Pile onto a double-thick layer of plastic wrap and roll up the butter into a thick roll about 1in (2.5cm) thick. Wrap tightly and chill for at least 30 minutes until you are ready to use it.

Herb and shallot butter

Makes approx. ½ cup (100g)

¾ stick (90g) **unsalted butter, softened**
1 **small shallot,** finely chopped
1 Tbsp **finely chopped fresh parsley**
1 Tbsp **finely chopped fresh chives**
Salt and freshly ground black pepper

Combine all the ingredients together in a small bowl until well mixed. Pile onto
a double-thick layer of plastic wrap and roll up the butter into a thick roll about 1in
(2.5cm) thick. Wrap tightly and chill for at least 30 minutes until you are ready to use it.

■ *Soft-leaved herbs work best for this butter. Other herbs to try are chopped dill or sage.*

Curried butter with dried apricots

Makes approx. ½ cup (100g)

¾ stick (90g) **unsalted butter, softened**
1 tsp **mild curry powder**
2 **no-soak dried apricots,** very finely chopped
Salt and freshly ground black pepper

Combine all the ingredients together in a small bowl until well mixed. Pile onto a double-
thick layer of plastic wrap and roll up the butter into a thick roll about 1in (2.5cm) thick.
Wrap tightly and chill for at least 30 minutes until you are ready to use it.

■ *For a spicier flavor add ¼–½ tsp chilli powder.*

Fresh mixed berry coulis

Makes approx. 2 cups (450ml)

½ cup (125g) **strawberries,** hulled
½ cup (125g) **raspberries,** defrosted if frozen
½ cup (125g) **blackberries,** defrosted if frozen
6 Tbsp **unsweetened apple juice**
1–2 Tbsp **maple syrup to taste**

Place all the fruit in a blender or food processor and add the apple juice. Blend for a few seconds until smooth. Put through a nylon sieve, if preferred, and add maple syrup to taste. Cover and chill until required.

■ *This coulis separates on standing, so stir well before serving.*

Tropical fruit coulis

Makes approx. 2 cups (450ml)

1 **small ripe mango**
½ **small ripe papaya**
1 **ripe kiwi fruit,** peeled and roughly chopped
6 Tbsp **unsweetened pineapple juice**
1–2 tsp **runny honey**

Peel the mango and slice down either side of the smooth flat central stone. Discard the stone, chop the flesh and put in a blender or food processor. Scoop out the seeds from the papaya and peel away the skin. Chop the flesh and add to the mango along with the kiwi fruit and pineapple juice. Blend for a few seconds until smooth. Add honey to taste, cover and chill until required.

■ *This coulis separates on standing, so stir well before serving.*

Butterscotch sauce

Makes approx. 2 cups (450ml)

⅔ cup (150g) **corn syrup**
½ stick (60g) **unsalted butter**
Scant 1 cup (150g) **demerara or light brown sugar**
⅔ cup (150ml) **heavy cream**
Few drops **vanilla extract**

Put the syrup, butter and sugar in a saucepan and heat gently, stirring, until dissolved. Bring to a simmer and cook gently for a further 5 minutes. Remove from the heat and gradually stir in the cream and vanilla extract. Serve hot or cold.

Chocolate sauce

Makes approx. 1¼ cups (300ml)

6oz (180g) **continental plain chocolate,** broken into pieces
1 Tbsp (15g) **unsalted butter**
6 Tbsp **heavy cream**
3 Tbsp **corn syrup**
Few drops **vanilla extract (optional)**

Put all the ingredients except the vanilla extract in a small heatproof bowl. Stand the bowl over a pan of gently simmering water and heat gently, stirring occasionally, until all the ingredients have melted together and the sauce is warm. Add a few drops of vanilla extract before serving. Serve warm – the sauce will harden on cooling.

■ *For a sauce that is less dark, use ordinary plain chocolate. For milk and white chocolate sauces, melt equal quantities of chocolate and double cream.*

Sweet vanilla custard sauce

Makes approx. 2½ cups (600ml)

3 Tbsp **cornstarch**
3 Tbsp **extra-fine sugar**
2½ cups (600ml) **milk**
2 **egg yolks**
Few drops **vanilla extract**
Few drops **yellow food coloring (optional)**

Blend the cornstarch and sugar in a saucepan with a little of the milk to form a paste. Heat the remaining milk to boiling point and stir in the cornstarch paste. Bring back to a boil, still stirring, and cook for 2 minutes until thick and glossy.

Set aside for 10 minutes, then stir in the egg yolks. Return to a gentle heat and cook through for a further 3 minutes without boiling. Add vanilla extract to taste, and the food coloring if using, and serve hot. If you want to serve the sauce cold, pour into a heatproof bowl and cover the surface with damp greaseproof paper to prevent a skin forming. Cool completely and store in the fridge until required.

■ *For a thick sauce, use ½ extra Tbsp cornstarch.*

Pesto sauce

Makes approx. ⅔ cup (150ml)

1 **clove garlic,** peeled and chopped
Generous ½ cup (15g) **fresh basil**
½ cup (60g) **pine nuts**
½ cup (60g) **finely grated fresh Parmesan cheese**
½ tsp **salt**
6 Tbsp **extra virgin olive oil**

Place all the ingredients in a blender or food processor and blend together until smooth and thick. Store in a sealed jar in the fridge for up to 5 days.

■ *For different flavors try these variations: replace the pine nuts with walnuts, pecans, almonds or hazelnuts. Parsley, watercress or arugula make a more peppery pesto, while cilantro gives an earthier flavor. For a healthy version, replace some or all of the olive oil with low-fat yogurt – this pesto will only keep for 2–3 days.*

Cheesy avocado relish

Serves 4

2 ripe medium avocados
Juice of 1 lime
4oz (125g) mature Cheddar cheese, grated
2 pickled jalapeños, drained and finely chopped
2 spring onions, trimmed and finely chopped
1 small bunch cilantro, finely chopped
6 Tbsp low-fat plain yogurt
Salt and freshly ground black pepper

Halve the avocados and remove the central stone. Peel the skin away and chop the flesh finely. If the avocados are too ripe, scoop out the flesh and lightly mash. Mix with the lime juice to prevent browning.

Carefully mix in the remaining ingredients, cover and chill for a maximum of about 30 minutes before serving.

Pineapple and red pepper relish

Serves 4

4 slices fresh pineapple, skinned, cored and finely chopped
1 large red pepper, deseeded and finely chopped
1 small red chilli, deseeded and finely chopped
2 Tbsp freshly chopped chives
2 Tbsp ready-made vinaigrette

Mix all the ingredients together, cover and chill until required.

Mango, red onion and tomato salsa

Serves 4

1 **medium red onion**, peeled and finely chopped
1 Tbsp **red wine vinegar**
1 **large mango**
2 **beef tomatoes**, finely chopped
2 Tbsp **finely chopped fresh cilantro**
3 Tbsp **smooth mango chutney**
1 Tbsp **sunflower oil**
Salt and freshly ground black pepper

Put the onion in a bowl and mix in the vinegar. Peel the mango and slice down either side of the smooth, flat central stone. Discard the stone and chop the flesh into small pieces; place in the bowl.

Mix in the remaining ingredients, cover and chill until required.

Sweet carrot and ginger chutney

Serves 4

2 large carrots, peeled and grated
4 spring onions, trimmed and finely chopped
1-in (2.5-cm) piece fresh ginger, peeled and grated
2 Tbsp toasted sesame seeds
2 Tbsp dry-roasted peanuts, crushed
2 Tbsp white rice vinegar or wine vinegar
4 tsp runny honey
2 tsp sesame seed oil
Salt and freshly ground black pepper

Mix all the ingredients together, cover and chill until required.

Tomato, black olive, garlic and basil salsa

Serves 4

4 **beef tomatoes**, finely chopped
½ cup (125g) **stoned black olives in brine,** drained and finely chopped
2 **cloves garlic,** peeled and finely chopped
Few sprigs **fresh basil,** finely chopped
2 Tbsp **extra virgin olive oil**
2 Tbsp **balsamic vinegar**
Salt and freshly ground black pepper

Mix all the ingredients together, cover and chill until required.

Roasted spiced vegetable chutney

Serves 4–6

1 **small yellow pepper,** deseeded and chopped
1 **small red pepper,** deseeded and chopped
1 **medium zucchini,** trimmed and chopped
2 **baby eggplants,** trimmed and chopped
4 Tbsp **olive oil**
Salt and freshly ground black pepper
2 **cloves garlic,** finely chopped
1 **beef tomato,** finely chopped
2 Tbsp **red wine vinegar**
1 Tbsp **runny honey**
1 tsp **ground cumin**

Preheat the oven to 400°F/200°C. Line a baking sheet with baking parchment and spread the vegetables over the sheet. Drizzle with 2 Tbsp olive oil and season well. Bake in the oven for about 25 minutes until tender and golden. Set aside to cool.

In a large bowl, mix together the remaining ingredients and add the cooled vegetables. Cover and chill until required.

Sweet and sour vegetable chutney

Serves 4

2 **slices fresh pineapple,** skinned, cored and finely chopped
1 **small red pepper,** deseeded and finely chopped
1 **small green pepper,** deseeded and finely chopped
4 **spring onions,** trimmed and finely chopped
1 **medium carrot,** peeled and grated
¼ cup (60g) **beansprouts**
3 Tbsp **unsweetened pineapple juice**
1 Tbsp **white rice vinegar or wine vinegar**
2 tsp **tomato purée**
2 tsp **light soy sauce**
1 tsp **runny honey**

Mix all the ingredients together, cover and chill until required.

Pickled cucumber and caper relish

Serves 4

½ **cucumber,** finely diced
1 **dill pickle,** finely chopped
1 **small onion,** peeled and finely chopped
2 Tbsp **small capers in brine,** drained
2 Tbsp **finely chopped parsley**
2 Tbsp **finely chopped dill**
2 Tbsp **ready-made vinaigrette**

Mix all the ingredients together, cover and chill until required.

About the author

Kathryn Hawkins is an experienced food writer and stylist. She has worked on several women's magazines on the full-time staff and now as a freelancer. Kathryn recently moved to Scotland from London, and now works from her beautiful Victorian guesthouse. She plans to open a cooking school and run residential and one-day culinary workshops in the house.

Kathryn enjoys using local produce in her cooking and writes on a wide range of cooking subjects. Her special interests include casual dining, regional food, cakes and baking, kid's cooking, food for health and healthy eating. Kathryn has been writing cookbooks for over a decade and has written several books on healthy eating.

Index